CRITICAL PERSPECTIVES ON
GUN CONTROL

ANALYZING THE ISSUES

CRITICAL PERSPECTIVES ON
GUN CONTROL

Edited by Anne C. Cunningham

Enslow Publishing
101 W. 23rd Street
Suite 240
New York, NY 10011
USA

enslow.com

Published in 2017 by Enslow Publishing, LLC
101 W. 23rd Street, Suite 240, New York, NY 10011

Cataloging-in-Publication Data

Names: Cunningham, Anne C., editor.
Title: Critical perspectives on gun control / edited by Anne C. Cunningham.
Description: New York : Enslow Publishing, 2017. | Series: Analyzing the issues |
Includes bibliographical references and index.
Identifiers: ISBN 9780766081253 (library bound)
Subjects: LCSH: Gun control—United States—Juvenile literature. | Firearms—
Law and legislation—United States—Juvenile literature. | Violent crimes—United States—Juvenile literature. | Firearms ownership—Government policy—
United States—Juvenile literature.
Classification: LCC HV7436.C746 2017 | DDC 363.330973—dc23

Printed in the United States of America

To Our Readers: We have done our best to make sure all website addresses in this book were active and appropriate when we went to press. However, the author and the publisher have no control over and assume no liability for the material available on those websites or on any websites they may link to. Any comments or suggestions can be sent by e-mail to customerservice@enslow.com.

Excerpts and articles have been reproduced with the permission of the copyright holders.

Photo Credits: Cover, STILLFX/Shutterstock.com (gun on US flag), Thaiview/Shutterstock.com (background, pp. 6–7 background), gbreezy/Shutterstock.com (magnifying glass on spine); p. 6 Ghornstern/Shutterstock.com (header design element, chapter start background throughout book.

CONTENTS

INTRODUCTION

The right to keep and bear arms for self-defense is a deeply cherished and constitutionally protected right in America. This freedom is bound up with fundamental American beliefs such as private property and individualism. Thus, it should come as no surprise that the cost of elevating gun rights to a sacred principle is an increasingly violent society. Is the tradeoff worth it?

This basic question, along with many others pertaining to the nuances of gun law, advocacy, and public opinion will comprise the chapters of this reader. Whatever your opinion on guns, it should be clear from the outset that America's relationship to them is highly emotional. And as sometimes happens with subjects that inspire much passion, misinformation and half-truths abound. It is our aim here to cut through this noise, and arrive at a balanced account of today's gun debate in America.

Prior to our discussion of gun control, a look at the rates of gun ownership and violence in the United States compared to other nations shall provide some context. The US boasts the title of most firearms per capita—an unbelievable 88.8 per 100 people when last measured in 2007! That is more than twice as many guns per 100 people as Norway, the nation that ranks second. And make no mistake—Americans are using these guns. Among developed nations, the US homicide rate is highest, at more than 3 per 100,000 people. These figures do not account for the near

12,000 suicides and accidental deaths in 2014 from guns. To provide additional perspective, in 2014, more people died in the US from the accidental discharge of a weapon than the total amount of homicides in the UK, Australia, and Japan combined.

Still, some remain unconvinced we have a problem with guns, and point to the fact that gun murder rates have actually decreased since their high in the early 1990s. While this is true, it fails to alter our place as the developed nation with the highest rate of gun violence. Buttressed by the Bill of Rights, a well-funded and vocal minority believes that there should be no compromises or restrictions on guns whatsoever, and that ownership is a birthright. However, as many scholars point out, gun control is also as old as the Second Amendment. Though the Second Amendment will no doubt survive legal challenges, Supreme Court decisions do allow much leeway for state and municipal gun laws.

Despite grim statistics, a majority of Americans also support some forms of gun control. What do we mean by gun control? These are local and state ordinances that determine one's legal right to purchase a firearm, the types of guns, ammunition, and paraphernalia that are considered to be in "common use" and therefore protected by the Second Amendment, and where and when these weapons can be carried and used. The key word in the above sentence is "attempt." Gun laws are notoriously easy to circumvent. As many gun rights supporters point out, those engaged in criminal activity do not care much for laws, while those who need a gun for protection are more vulnerable if access to guns is limited. While this argument contains a shred of truth, few would insist that this renders moot the goal of keeping weapons out of the hands of those with violent criminal backgrounds, suspected terrorists on no-fly lists, or the mentally ill.

On the gun rights side, one salient point bears highlighting. The systematic disarming of segments of the population, notably slaves and later freed African Americans, is part of our nation's history. For this reason, we should be wary of an uncritical discourse of "criminality." Enforced incorrectly, new gun laws could entangle more people in the criminal justice system, especially urban minorities. This could feed the prison-industrial complex. One can easily imagine a young man with a minor narcotics infraction on his record going to jail for having a gun, especially if such an individual lacks legal representation. In this scenario, gun arrests and prosecutions could become analogous to crack cocaine charges. These laws yielded stiff mandatory minimum sentences that were quite unfairly racially biased.

Finally, a word on mass shootings: these sensational events tend to skew the gun issue back to the aforementioned (and distorting) emotional plane. Since mass shootings constitute a small fraction of overall gun deaths, it is more fruitful to approach this horrifying phenomenon as a mental health and sociological issue.

CHAPTER 1

WHAT THE EXPERTS SAY

It is tempting to write off gun enthusiasts as dogmatic, unenlightened extremists. To the multitudes of Americans horrified by increasingly commonplace gun tragedies, gun-rights advocates willfully obstruct our progress toward a more peaceful social order. Why would anyone wish to sacrifice a less deadly society for an abstract (and possibly moribund) principle based upon a centuries-old document?

Upon closer scrutiny, the debate over gun rights becomes slightly more complex. True, common sense dictates that fewer guns mean less gun crimes. Even among National Rifle Association (NRA) members, support for universal background checks is rising. Surprisingly though, there is no correlation between a state's gun laws and its rate of gun crimes. For example, Vermont has one of the most permissive gun cultures in the United States, but consistently has the lowest rate of gun violence.

Experts conclude that the effect of new gun legislation on crime would be moderate at best. Still, why would we delay putting even moderately successful laws into place if they save lives?

The Second Amendment of the Constitution guarantees a citizen's right to self-defense, but like other amendments, is subject to conditions and restrictions. The nature of these restrictions is the terrain upon which gun control debate plays out. As we'll see, attempts to disarm segments of the population have often served a racist agenda throughout US history. For this reason, we might wish to interrogate the precise criteria by which one is defined as a "criminal."

"FEWER GUNS, LESS HOMICIDE? IF ONLY IT WERE SO SIMPLE," BY ROBERT VERBRUGGEN, FROM *NATIONAL REVIEW*, DEC. 21, 2015

The United States has a much higher homicide rate than just about any other highly developed country, and it also has much more civilian gun ownership. Further, within the U.S., the simplest analysis — the type journalists can do, using data that are readily available online — reveals tight correlations between states' gun deaths and factors such as gun ownership and gun-control laws. The obvious conclusion seems to be: Get rid of the guns, get rid of the violence. It's that simple, everyone knows it, and yet redneck conservatives in thrall to the NRA stubbornly resist handing over their weapons.

That's a seductive line of reasoning — especially in the wake of horrifying, high-profile incidents such as the recent mass shooting in Colorado Springs — but it's false. In fact, the United States' overall high rate of homicide is largely explained, perhaps entirely explained, by problems unrelated to gun ownership. There are policies concerning gun ownership that could reduce homicide, but the reductions would most likely be modest.

There is actually no simple correlation between states' *homicide* rates and their gun-ownership rates or gun laws. This has been shown numerous times, by different people, using different data sets. A year ago, I took state gun-ownership levels reported by the *Washington Post* (based on a Centers for Disease Control survey) and compared them with murder rates from the FBI: no correlation. The legal scholar Eugene Volokh has compared states' gun laws (as rated by the anti-gun Brady Campaign) with their murder rates: no correlation. David Freddoso of the *Washington Examiner*, a former National Review reporter, failed to find a correlation even between gun ownership in a state and gun murders specifically, an approach that sets aside the issue of whether gun availability has an effect on non-gun crime. (Guns can deter unarmed criminals, for instance, and criminals without guns may simply switch to other weapons.)

For good measure, I recently redid my analysis with a few tweaks. Instead of relying on a single year of survey data, I averaged three years. (The CDC survey, the best available for state-level numbers, included data on gun ownership only in 2001, 2002, and 2004. Those were the years I looked at.) And instead of comparing CDC data with murder rates from a different agency, I relied on the

CDC's own estimates of death by assault in those years. Again: no correlation.

Left-leaning media outlets, from *Mother Jones* to *National Journal*, get around this absence of correlation by reporting numbers on "gun deaths" rather than gun homicides or homicides in general. More than 60 percent of gun deaths nationally are suicides, and places with higher gun ownership typically see a higher percentage of their suicides committed with a gun. Focusing on the number of gun deaths practically guarantees a finding that guns and violence go together. While it may be true that public policy should also seek to reduce suicide, it is homicide — often a dramatic mass killing — that usually prompts the media and politicians to call for gun control, and it is homicide that most influences people as they consider supporting measures to take away their fellow citizens' access to guns.

There are large gaps among the states when it comes to homicide, with rates ranging all the way from about two to twelve per 100,000 in 2013, the most recent year of data available from the CDC. These disparities show that it's not just guns that cause the United States to have, on average, a higher rate of homicide than other developed countries do. Not only is there no correlation between gun ownership and overall homicide within a state, but there is a strong correlation between gun homicide and non-gun homicide — suggesting that they spring from similar causes, and that some states are simply more violent than others. A closer look at demographic and geographic patterns provides some clues as to why this is.

The first major factor is race. Blacks lacked the government's protection from violence through most of

American history and even today have higher rates of homicide than other racial groups do. Despite being 13 percent of the general population and owning guns at just half the rate of whites, blacks commit about half of murders, overwhelmingly against other blacks. Drawing on recent CDC data, the website FiveThirtyEight has reported that while blacks suffer homicide at a rate of 19.4 per 100,000, the rate for non-Hispanic whites is just 2.5 — "not so much of an outlier" in the international context, FiveThirtyEight notes. To the extent that the legacy of slavery and Jim Crow affects homicide rates among black Americans, it prevents meaningful comparisons with countries that lack a comparably lamentable racial history.

Race is not the end of the story, though, because a rate of 2.5 per 100,000 would still put America solidly above most of Western Europe, where rates tend to be around one per 100,000. Further differences become apparent when, in addition to focusing on the death rates of non-Hispanic whites, we break the CDC data down by state, combining the years 2009 through 2013 to make the rates more reliable at this more local level.

Whites in 14 states face a roughly European level of violence, with an annual homicide risk of no more than 1.5 per 100,000. Confusingly, these states don't appear to have much in common culturally. They include liberal states known for gang violence in poor minority areas (New York, New Jersey), mostly rural red states teeming with firearms (Idaho, North Dakota), Upper Midwest states with strong hunting cultures but also large urban areas (Wisconsin, Minnesota), and gun-loving states either purple (New Hampshire) or solidly blue (Vermont).

But there is, in fact, a common thread: They are all in the northern United States. Cognitive psychologist Steven Pinker, documenting this pattern in *The Better Angels of Our Nature*, ascribes differences in state violence to a North-South divide reflecting "historical routes of migration." He notes that "the Chesapeake colonies of Maryland and Virginia started out more violent than New England." As Pinker and countless others have discussed, inhabitants of the North were relatively quick to establish the rule of law and allow the government a monopoly on violence, while the South developed a "culture of honor" in which individuals took personal slights seriously and handled their disputes themselves, sometimes resorting to violence.

This difference suggests that there will be higher homicide rates in the South, regardless of the prevalence of guns. In fact, whites in the most violent states — mainly in the South and Southwest, where gun ownership is high — have *non-gun-assault* death rates around 1.5 to 2 per 100,000, enough to put them above the *total* rates of the least violent foreign nations and of white Americans in peaceful northern states. Similarly, to return to the previous topic, blacks nationwide have a rate of non-gun-assault death above 3.5 per 100,000.

Of course, it's possible that America's gun laws (which are permissive compared with those in Europe), while not fundamentally driving these broad patterns, are dumping gasoline onto racial and cultural fires. In one theory, for example, the Second Amendment is basically tangled up with everything else that's wrong with America. As the historian Jill Lepore once summarized it, in reviewing Pieter Spierenburg's *A History of Murder:*

By the time European states became democracies, the populace had accepted the authority of the state. But the American Revolution happened before Americans had got used to the idea of a state monopoly on force. Americans therefore preserved for themselves not only the right to bear arms — rather than yielding that right to a strong central government — but also medieval manners: impulsiveness, crudeness, and fidelity to a culture of honor. We're backward, in other words, because we became free before we learned how to control ourselves.

To assess more nuanced arguments, such as this one, we need an analysis that takes numerous variables into account and enables us to isolate the effect we're looking for. Do such analyses reliably find that, all else equal, an unarmed population is a safer one? Or do guns not make much of a difference — which might be the case if, for example, civilian guns deterred as much crime as they enabled, or if criminals without ready access to guns simply used other weapons instead?

You'd certainly get the impression that guns increase violence from reading public-health academic journals, which have been churning out findings along those lines for decades. Some of these studies are well done and worthy of consideration. But when we look beyond public-health studies and also consider the findings of economists and criminologists, the picture becomes a lot blurrier.

Recently, the criminologist Gary Kleck reviewed about 40 studies that probed the link between gun ownership and crime. These compared a wide range of geographies, from cities to entire nations. Half of the findings indicated a link tying guns to higher homicide rates; the other half found none. But the more rigorous a study was, the less likely it was to find such a correlation. "It must be tentatively concluded that higher gun ownership rates do not cause higher crime rates, including homicide rates," Kleck wrote.

Despite the impression left by a spate of media reports earlier this year, this finding is consistent with the experience of Australia, which confiscated about 20 percent of civilian-owned guns almost immediately following the passage of a 1996 law. This policy may have reduced suicide rates somewhat, but even the analysis of the program most often cited by liberals (from Australian economists Andrew Leigh and Christine Neill) is inconclusive as to its effect on firearm homicides, to say nothing of total homicides — and the basic homicide trend lines provided by the Australian government certainly don't reveal anything obvious. Similarly, in the U.K., the homicide rate actually rose shortly after the country enacted stricter gun controls, though it has since come back down.

It is very possible, then, that disarming the citizenry would do nothing at all to decrease homicide. Disarmament is also the policy least likely to garner political support in America, not to mention pass muster in any court honestly interpreting the Second Amendment. A much more promising idea is to focus on keeping guns out of the hands of criminals. Under current federal law, it is illegal for anyone to sell a gun knowing that the buyer is prohibited from having it. (Prohibited categories include felons, those convicted of certain domestic-violence misdemeanors, someone who is "an unlawful user of or addicted to a controlled substance," and those who've been involuntarily committed to a mental institution.) On top of that, licensed gun dealers are required to run background checks before making sales, and to keep records of sales for at least 20 years, but there are no such requirements for a private citizen selling a gun to a stranger. This is often called the "gun-show loophole," though it is not a loophole and has nothing to do with gun shows: It's simply what the law says, and the distinction between dealers and non-dealers applies whether the sale takes place at a gun show or not.

There are many proposals to reform this system. The most commonsensical ones focus on domestic violence and mental illness. Hillary Clinton, for example, would expand the list of misdemeanors that legally disqualify people from gun ownership to include domestic violence against a non-cohabiting partner, as well as stalking. A related proposal, heavily promoted by the Center for American Progress and enacted in some states, would strip gun rights from those under a temporary restraining order, which raises some due-process concerns because such orders are issued without a hearing. Mental-health records, meanwhile, are a disaster, with the names of too many dangerous people left out of the system that background checks rely on, a problem that President Obama has begun to address with an executive order. Mental-health reforms are especially promising when it comes to preventing suicides and mass shootings.

These ideas, while important, do not address the core of the gun-violence problem: male-on-male acts of aggression, largely by men with criminal records, sometimes quite extensive ones. Few career criminals get their guns from licensed dealers, where a background check would be run and records kept. Inmate surveys indicate that criminals overwhelmingly get their guns through social connections instead.

A recent study of 99 criminals facing weapons charges in the Chicago area revealed why they were more likely to have acquired guns through social connections than in private deals with strangers. Illicit gun sellers avoid doing business with strangers because they worry about being caught in a sting operation; buyers, meanwhile, are fearful of being sold a gun that has been used in a crime. Most of the guns that criminals use are old and change hands repeatedly, sometimes being borrowed rather than sold. However, legally purchased guns often quickly make their way to criminals; several inmates reported that gun suppliers bought weapons in stores, reported them stolen, and resold them.

These findings are a reality check. There are many, many guns already in circulation in the United States, and it would be incredibly difficult to impose background checks on criminal social networks. Our best hope is to stop guns from being diverted to the criminal market to begin with. And while background checks cannot stop people from reporting guns stolen that actually haven't been, they do seem to have an effect in the handful of states that have enacted them: Gangs are often forced to bring in guns from states without such restrictions. Criminals will not simply give up if background checks go nationwide, of course, but this does suggest that the policy affects behavior on the margins.

Polls indicate overwhelming support for universal background checks — with a majority in favor even among Republicans, gun owners, and NRA members. But the devil is in the details, and proposals face staunch opposition from NRA leaders. In the wake of the massacre at Sandy Hook Elementary School, even a relatively modest bill from Senators Pat Toomey and Joe Manchin fell flat on its face. (The authors are reportedly looking to bring the legislation back.) Here are the major tradeoffs such a scheme poses:

Which gun transfers require checks? Manchin-Toomey would have been limited to sales that took place at gun shows or were advertised online or in a publication — precisely the sales that criminals are already avoiding. A requirement of background checks in a broader swath of transfers, while difficult to enforce in real time and harder to sell politically, would aid the prosecution of those whose guns wind up in the hands of criminals. Under this approach, the simple act of transferring a gun without a check would be a crime; by contrast, today, prosecutors need to prove that someone deliberately sold to a prohibited person or served as a "straw purchaser," passing a background check and buying a gun on someone else's behalf. Other tricky issues include how to permit inheritances, gifts, and the temporary borrowing of guns among family and friends without creating loopholes or making criminals of innocent people. (For a detailed discussion of how this might be achieved, search online for David Kopel's new law-review article "Background Checks for Firearms Sales and Loans: Law, History, and Policy.")

Are records kept? Under Manchin-Toomey, gun dealers conducting checks on behalf of private sellers would have kept records the same way they do when selling their own inventory — but this was a major point of contention during the debate in Congress. Without records of these sales, police would have less of a paper trail to follow. The objection to keeping such records is that they constitute a de facto gun registry, albeit a scattered one, that the government could use to track down and confiscate legally purchased firearms. This seems rather unlikely, but, in fairness, gun confiscation has happened in other modern Anglosphere nations: Australia, the U.K., and Canada.

Who keeps the records? Currently, records are spread through countless gun stores, and getting to them involves tracing the gun through manufacturers, importers, and wholesalers. When stores go out of business, their records are transferred to the federal government, which must not organize them into a searchable database because doing so would create a registry (which would be illegal under current federal law). All this would become even more complicated with private sales in the mix — different sales of a gun would be documented at different stores, and the gun's various owners would need to point police to each new dealer. One solution would be to have gun manufacturers, rather than stores, keep track of who has purchased their guns: If the gun is a Ruger, Ruger has its records. Another would be for stores to report the serial numbers of the guns they've sold, but not the buyers' information, to a searchable federal data-base. This would quickly point investigators to the correct gun store without compromising the privacy of those not under investigation. (It's similar to a requirement already in place regarding used guns sold by dealers who are consid-ered high-risk.) Of course, these approaches would heighten concerns about a registry.

Who pays? Manchin-Toomey would have allowed those conducting the checks to charge fees. If the government decides to require these checks of people exercising a constitutional right, perhaps it should pick up the tab.

In my opinion, a background check — provided it's free and convenient — is not too much to ask of someone buying or selling a gun, and I am not particularly troubled by the prospect of a "registry" held by private businesses. But background checks will not be the ultimate solution to our homicide problem. They may not even be worth the considerable expense. America has a high rate of homicide relative to similar countries, and reducing that rate is a laudable and pressing goal. But preventing violence is a far more difficult and complicated task than many would have us think.

1. This article questions the link between rates of gun ownership and homicide, concluding that some states are simply more violent that others. Do you agree with this?

2. Those opposing gun control measures believe a searchable national gun registry would represent an invasion of privacy rights. However, such a database could also help prosecute gun crimes as well as deter guns from falling into the wrong hands. How do you see this tradeoff between privacy and public safety? Where along this spectrum do your views fall?

"GUYS WITH GUNS: THE U.S. GOVERNMENT SHOULD BE MAKING IT MORE DIFFICULT TO SELL WEAPONS—AT HOME AS WELL AS ABROAD," BY JOHN FEFFER, FROM *FOREIGN POLICY IN FOCUS*, JUNE 18, 2014

Back in the 1950s, the far right-wing John Birch Society worried that Communists were secretly behind the fluoridation of the American drinking water. This particular conspiracy theory probably would have vanished into collective amnesia if it hadn't been so pointedly satirized—and thus immortalized—in the film *Dr. Strangelove.*

I have to say, however, that I am tempted by such crackpot notions when confronted by the heart-breaking headlines these days. The violence that is escalating all around us seems to defy explanation. All I can think is that someone has dumped a different substance, testosterone, into our drinking water. How else to explain all the recent shootings, including ones by a frustrated virgin at UC Santa Barbara, an extremist couple in Las Vegas, and an ultra-religious teenager outside of Portland, Oregon?

According to the FBI, the United States experienced five mass killings a year between 2000 and 2008. Since 2009, however, we've gone up to 16 such killings a year. The FBI defines a "mass killing" as an incident in which more than four people are killed. The Las Vegas and Portland killings don't even qualify.

Since the shooters all seem to act from different motives, it's hard to come up with a single explanation for this rising tide of violence. Perhaps it's just the convergence of massive amounts of weaponry, loose gun laws, a broken mental health system, ultraviolent video games and TV shows, and rising anti-government sentiment. Perhaps by some law of conservation of violence, the United States draws down its large-scale military engagements overseas and the aggression rises on the home front. Perhaps it's just the copycat element.

But there's considerable appeal in a crackpot theory that allows you to believe that everything is fine with society, except for one evil group of people (the Koch brothers), one malign institution (the NRA), or one dastardly act (pumping a male sex hormone associated with uncontrollable anger into the drinking supply).

Of course, it's not just the United States. Someone has obviously been putting something into the water in eastern Ukraine as well. There was a striking photo in *The Washington Post* a few weeks ago. It showed a group of pro-Russian sympathizers at a rally in eastern Ukraine. There wasn't a woman in sight. And nearly all the men had the same male-pattern baldness—characteristic of high levels of testosterone.

Perhaps Russian President Vladimir Putin himself, who seems to have a private stash of the stuff, ordered the male sex hormone to be dumped into the drinking water of eastern Ukraine (along with dispatching mercenaries, material, and money to help the separatists). What started out as an almost comical uprising of the disgruntled has turned into a bloody civil war.

With the death toll rising into the hundreds, the new Ukrainian president Petro Poroshenko has vowed to pursue peace negotiations with the rebels. But first he wants to secure the borders. Russia has offered its own ceasefire plan at the UN. And on the ground, fighting has damaged a pumping station in Donestsk, threatening the water supply to 4 million people. Whatever's in the water, there might be a whole lot less of it very soon, precipitating a humanitarian crisis.

All along the Russian-leaning separatists in Ukraine have called into question the legitimacy of the government in Kiev. When they occupied buildings in eastern Ukraine, they compared their actions to what the protestors in Kiev had done to oust the corrupt president, Viktor Yanukovych.

This is a false equivalence. Among the many differences between what is taking place now in eastern Ukraine and what took place back in February in the capital city, the biggest has to do with gender and guns. The Euromaidan protestors included a large number of women—older women holding signs that read simply "Mama," younger women who took to Twitter and YouTube to build support, even a women's self-defense unit—and it was predominantly (though not exclusively) non-violent. The separatists in the east are armed, and they are predominantly men.

The imbalance is only growing. Women and children are fleeing the fighting in eastern Ukraine. It's not so easy for the men to go, however. "It's hard for the men to get out," one of the escaping women told *The Washington Post.* "The Donetsk People's Republic say women and children can go. But they pull men off the buses and say they should stay to protect Slovyansk."

Meanwhile in Iraq, the guys with guns are really going at it. The extremist group ISIL (Islamic State of Iraq and Levant—elsewhere rendered ISIS, for the Islamic State of Iraq and Syria) has taken over a large swath of northern Iraq and begun to merge it with the sections of Syria that it controls. These particular militants are purists on the issue of gender and violence. The Sunni gunmen of ISIL are exclusively male and committed to using violence to secure as much territory as possible for their mini-caliphate. According to the rules ISIL has disseminated, women must stay at home, unless absolutely necessary. Shia militias have quickly mobilized volunteers to defend Baghdad and other Shia-dominated areas as Iraq finally fractures along sectarian lines. Expect a stalemate as one set of guys with guns squares off against another set of guys with guns.

And the biggest guy with a gun of them all, the U.S. government, is contemplating air strikes against ISIL. An aircraft carrier is in position, and the Pentagon can draw on air power at bases in Qatar, Kuwait, and elsewhere. Although ISIL is a horrifying group of guys with guns, air strikes will likely be ineffective. It's very difficult to attack a group of irregulars who can blend in with the population. So, air strikes will likely result in large numbers of civilian casualties, which would only swell the number of potential recruits for ISIL.

It's always tempting to drink whatever they're drinking—but the Obama administration should just politely refuse. Defining ISIL not as terrorists bent on attacking the United States but, rather, a "sectarian militia waging a civil war, puts the emphasis on where it needs to be: finding an integrated political-military solution to the internal Iraqi problems that sparked the civil war," writes Kenneth Pollack at Brookings. "And that is a set of problems that is unlikely to be solved by immediate, direct American attacks on the Sunni militants."

Sending more guys with guns into a situation dominated by guys with guns is a recipe for failure, as the military interventions in Afghanistan and Iraq have amply demonstrated. The Obama administration seems to have learned that lesson to some extent. No U.S. ground troops are slated for Iraq or Ukraine (though Washington is sending a contingent to protect the U.S. embassy in Baghdad and has promised more military presence in Europe as a deterrent). But the administration must endure the pleadings from both right and center to "do something." Diplomacy is never seen as doing something. Doing something almost always seems to involve guys with guns.

As with gun violence on the home front, the United States should be pursuing an obvious policy: reduce the number of guns going into the hands of guys. But the obvious policy is not so obvious to those in power (or, in the case of the arms lobby, those *with* power). The best we've managed are some regulations that affect the flow of arms in marginal ways. At home, you have to go through a background check—though people who would obviously fail such a check can just go to a gun show in most states and buy a weapon there.

Abroad, we have the Leahy Law, a 1997 initiative to stop the flow of U.S. arms to known human rights viola-tors. The law is an admirable effort to apply a kind of background check to all the many would-be purchasers of U.S. weapons. It has only been successfully applied to a minority of cases—less than 1 percent of all candidates for assistance.

As with domestic gun control legislation, even the modest Leahy Law has generated pushback from the suppliers. The latest case involves the Nigerian army, which the Pentagon wants to help go after that other group of guys with guns, Boko Haram, the extremist organization that continues to hold on to a couple hundred schoolgirls it abducted more than two months ago. Chairman of the House Foreign Affairs Committee Ed Royce recently called for a waiver of the Leahy Law so that the United States could provide more assistance to the Nigerian military. He cited the U.S. military's complains of the law's restrictions. The Pentagon replied that it was actually criticizing the Nigerian military's human rights violations. But the uncomfortable fact is that the Pentagon has indeed publicly complained over having its hands tied.

Another effort to rein in guys with guns has been to reduce the prevalence of wartime rape. A number of world leaders, including Secretary of State John Kerry, convened last week in London to talk about how to prevent rape in conflict. Organizers want, among other things, to establish an international protocol for documenting and investigating sexual violence in conflict zones.

But Musimbi Kanyoro and Serra Sippel, writing in Foreign Policy In Focus this week, point out that the U.S. government can address the problem right away by changing or repealing the Helms amendment, which has been used to prohibit any U.S. funding for abortions overseas. "As a result, most organizations that rely on U.S. aid too often turn their backs when pregnant rape survivors ask for help," they write. "Those health providers are afraid to lose their funding and therefore avoid abortion services and referrals altogether."

Aside from the relatively modest fixes—strengthen the Leahy Law and deep-six the Helms amendment—what can the United States do to address all this violence?

We've had wars on drugs, on poverty, on cancer. We've had so many such wars that even our metaphors are now locked and loaded. Meanwhile, the guys with guns continue to wage their very real wars at home and abroad. Before we retire "war as metaphor," however, we should wage one last conflict: a war on guns.

If we can have zero tolerance for poverty, surely we can mobilize the public behind zero tolerance for assault weapons. We won't be able to eliminate murder— Cain didn't need a semi-automatic to kill his brother—but we'll surely reduce *mass* murder. Even if someone does manage to slip steroids into the water supply, male rage will not result in large-scale, indiscriminate killing. The same should apply to our arms export policy. The government should be making it more difficult to sell weapons overseas—not facilitating those exports, as the Obama administration has done.

Our bodily fluids are indeed precious, as General Jack D. Ripper says in *Dr. Strangelove*. It's just too bad we've made it so easy to acquire the guns that can be used to spill those fluids.

1. What do you think about the link the author draws between gender and gun violence? Does this validate or invalidate his main argument?

"HOW GUN CONTROL HURTS MINORITIES: PROGRESSIVES TURN THEIR BACKS ON THOSE MOST VULNERABLE TO EXPANDED POLICE POWERS," BY MEG ARNOLD AND NATHAN GOODMAN, *PANAM POST*, OCTOBER 13, 2015

In the wake of the tragic mass shooting at Oregon's Umpqua Community College, many commentators and politicians are calling for stricter gun control.

Hillary Clinton promises to take administrative action if Congress refuses to expand federal background checks to all gun sales. Likewise, Bernie Sanders is sure to upset some of his constituents when he rolls out his new gun policy in response to this tragedy.

But restricting liberties in the wake of a crisis will only cause more harm. Laws passed in reaction to a crisis often provide the impetus for substantial expansions of state power. There is occasionally some retrenchment afterwards, but the state always remains larger and more powerful than it was before.

After 9/11, the US government launched dramatic assaults on privacy, habeas corpus, and other basic civil liberties. Likewise, the Great Depression enabled erosions of economic liberty that we still live with today, including crony-capitalist boondoggles like the Export-Import Bank and farm subsidies.

We shouldn't allow tragic mass shootings to provide excuses for expanding government power and restricting individual liberties.

Defending gun rights is often seen as a conservative project, but it shouldn't be. Many progressives recognize that the criminal justice system unjustly and unfairly harms the poorest and most marginalized in our society. That same criminal justice system is responsible for enforcing gun control, and the results are tragically predictable.

Gun-control advocates want to solve the problems of gun violence, but they forget that the state uses violence to enforce the laws that they advocate.

Dean Spade, an associate professor of law at Seattle University and the founder of the Sylvia Rivera Law Project, notes: "When we have a conversation about gun violence that ignores the realities of state violence, it often produces proposals that further marginalize and criminalize people of color, poor people, people with disabilities, and youth."

Racism is not merely a byproduct of gun control when racist individuals do the enforcing; racism is inherent to gun control in a systemic way.

The United States enacted its first gun-control policies to disarm indigenous people and recently freed slaves. Later laws sought to prevent the Black Panthers from openly carrying firearms.

Recent gun-control initiatives may lack racist intent, but they nevertheless inflict racially disparate consequences. New York implemented its stop-and-frisk policy, which enabled the New York Police Department to harass and profile people of color, in the name of getting weapons off the streets.

There are similar disparities on a national level. Anthony Gregory of the Independent Institute notes that in 2011, "49.6 percent of those sentenced to federal incarceration with a primary offense of firearms violations were black, 20.6 percent were Hispanic, and only 27.5 percent were white."

Many gun-control laws feature mandatory-minimum sentences. This prevents judges from considering specific circumstances while sentencing, and thus requires disproportionate and unjust prison terms.

Mandatory minimums allow prosecutors to stack charges. Defendants then face decades of imprisonment if convicted, and can be intimidated into accepting plea bargains, rather than exercising their right to trial by jury.

The right to bear arms often comes up as a defense against government power and as a means for the people to cast off oppressive rule. Gun-control laws tend to disarm those who are already most oppressed. Worse, they give the state further pretexts to harass, surveil, and jail marginalized people.

Everyone who cares about liberty, justice, or equality, should be skeptical of calls for harsher gun control.

1. Do you think criminal background checks and other restrictions on gun ownership might be tacitly racist in practice? Explain your answer.

2. If you answered "yes" above, how might we balance this potentially racist problem against the legitimate risk of weapons falling into dangerous hands? Which takes precedence, in your opinion?

EXCERPT FROM "RACISM, GUN OWNERSHIP AND GUN CONTROL: BIASED ATTITUDES IN US WHITES MAY INFLUENCE POLICY DECISIONS," BY KERRY O'BRIEN, WALTER FORREST, DERMOT LYNOTT, AND MICHAEL DALY, FROM *PLOS ONE*, OCTOBER 13, 2012

INTRODUCTION

Several mass shootings in 2012 (e.g., Sandy Hook Elementary School, Connecticut; Aurora, Colorado) reignited gun-control and firearm ownership debates in the United States (US). The public health importance of gun reform in the US is clear and should not need such tragedies for policy change. In 2011, there were 32,163 firearm-related deaths in the US, with 11,101 homicides (69.5% of all homicides), and 19,776 suicides (51.6% of all suicides) [1]. Rates of firearm homicides in the US (3.6 per 100,000) are over 7-fold of those in similar nations (e.g., Canada, 0.5; United Kingdom, 0.1; Australia, 0.1) [2]. Blacks are disproportionately represented in US firearm homicides (14.6 per 100,000), and would benefit most from improved gun controls [1]. Opposition to gun control is considerably stronger in whites than blacks [3], with whites also reporting twice the rate of personal gun ownership and having a gun in the home, than is reported by blacks [4]. Proponents of gun-ownership rights cite self-protection and safety as their primary argument for owning guns and resisting gun reform [4, 5]. This is paradoxical, as whites, and particularly white males, are considerably more likely to commit suicide with firearms (7.3 and 12.9 per 100,000, respectively), than die from a firearm homicide (1.9 per 100,000) [1]. Indeed, US research found that having one or more guns in the home is related to a 2.7 and 4.8 fold increase in the risk of a member of that household dying from homicide or suicide, respectively [6, 7]. Given that gun controls have been shown to reduce suicides and homicides [8–10] arguments against gun reform based on self-defense/protection/safety are counterintuitive, and are inhibiting the adoption of appropriate policy to improve public health. As such, it is important for public health advocates, researchers, and policy makers to consider all explanations for opposition to gun reform in US whites. However, research on the reasons for opposition to gun control is sparse, in part because of restrictions on funding for research on gun control in the US [11, 12].

Stronger opposition to gun control by US whites has not always been the case. During the civil rights movement of the late 60 s, black activists exercised their right to carry loaded firearms in order to provide protection from police and extreme white factions [13]. The response from US whites was to demand stricter gun control. The Mulford Act was signed into law by Californian governor Ronald Reagan in 1967, and prohibited the carrying of loaded firearms in public [13]. The social landscape has changed considerably, and most recent data indicates a quite different view on gun control by whites, with 53% of whites wanting to protect the right to own guns, whereas only 24% of blacks do [14].

People's stated reasons for owning guns and opposing gun-control legislation are likely complex; however, it has been suggested that sociocultural factors such as fear of black violence may be associated with gun ownership, and with opposition to gun controls [15, 16]. Similarly, negative attitudes towards blacks (i.e., racism), along with conservative and political ideologies, appear to be related to fear of black violence and crime [17–20]. What is not known, and accordingly is the focus of this study, is whether racism is associated with gun owner- ship and opposition to gun control. It has been found that racial stereotypes (e.g., that blacks are violent) are related to US whites' fears of violence from blacks, and to their support for crime-related policy measures, such as building prisons, and the death penalty [19, 20]. Support for such policies is particularly pronounced in US whites who hold higher levels of racism [19]. Strong evidence also supports the notion that negative racial stereo- types and attitudes are related to people's perceptions of threat from black gun-related violence [20]. Additionally, US research using measures of implicit race attitudes (e.g., Implicit Association Test; IAT) have shown a prefer- ence for whites over blacks [21] and appear to influence people's political decisions, and even choices of medical procedures for blacks [22–24]. For instance, measures of explicit and implicit racism measures predicted opposi- tion to Obama's health reforms [23].

Most prominently, symbolic racism (racial resent- ment), an explicit but subtle form and measure of racism, has been found to be consistently related to peoples decisions regarding policies that may affect non-white US citizens. It is argued that symbolic racism supplanted old-fashioned or overt/blatant racism which had seen blacks as amoral and inferior, and was associated with open support for race inequality and segregation under

'Jim Crow Laws' [25]. Research following the US civil-rights movement suggested that anti-black racism and stereotyping, as assessed by blatant measures, had declined [26]. However, subsequent research revealed that people may merely be reluctant to express racism and negative stereotyping on these blatant measures in order to avoid appearing racist [27, 28]. This observation led to the conceptualization and measurement of more subtle measures of racism, such as, symbolic racism [25].

Symbolic racism is a belief structure underpinned by both anti-black affect and traditional values [29]. The anti-black affect (racism) component of symbolic racism is said to be established in pre-adult years through exposure to negative black stereotypes (e.g. blacks as dangerous, blacks are lazy), to the point that phenomena such as crime and physical violence have become typi-fied as black phenomena [30]. The anti-black affect is not necessarily conscious or deliberative, but may be felt as fear, anger, unease, and hostility towards blacks [29, 31, 32]. The symbolic component reflects the abstract view of blacks as a collective rather than as individuals, as well as its basis in abstract white moralistic reasoning and traditions. Because symbolic racism represents an ingrained schema, individuals high in symbolic racism will react in a negative manner, often unconsciously, to issues perceived to involve a racial (i.e. black) component. Psychometric work shows that while symbolic racism has a small relationship with old-fashioned or blatant racism and stereotypes, only symbolic racism is associated with policy preferences related to race after controlling for conservative and political ideology and demographic characteristics (e.g., education, gender, age) [33].

Policies of which blacks or whites are the intended or obvious beneficiaries (e.g. affirmative action, school busing) should easily be perceived as involving a racial component. But other policies may also involve a perceived racial component merely because they concern an issue that is already understood by whites in racial (black) terms. Thus, symbolic racism has been linked to opposition to and support for a range of policies that whites consistently associate with blacks (e.g., welfare), even if it is not in the self-interest of whites to do so [22–25, 32]. This is also likely to explain the frequently observed correlations between symbolic racism and public opinion regarding a range of criminal justice policies (e.g. death penalty, mandatory sentences). There is substantial evidence that whites associate blacks with crime, and especially violent crime [19, 30]. The result of this conflation of race and crime is that whites high on symbolic racism will support policies that are perceived as being tough on crime and oppose policies that are considered lenient. Green and colleagues [34] have found a positive relationship between symbolic racism and punitive crime policies (i.e., death penalty, three strikes imprisonment), and negative correlation with policies that are intended to assist criminals (i.e., education of inmates, poverty reduction). And although conservative ideologies and racism are inherently related, symbolic racism makes a unique contribution to crime policy attitudes after accounting for other race-neutral factors (e.g., conservatism, crime victimization, crime news exposure, and socio-demographics) [34]. More generally, symbolic racism should also correlate with fear of crime and black violence, along with attitudes to policies that may reduce, or increase, perceived threat (e.g., gun ownership, gun control). Self-protection and physical safety (e.g., fear) are the most commonly cited reason for owning a gun and opposing gun control and blacks are overrepresented in the crime statistics and media portrayals of violent crime. Accordingly, people with higher symbolic racism may be more likely to own a gun and oppose gun control as a means of dealing (consciously or unconsciously) with abstract fears regarding blacks [19].

Given the importance of guns and gun-control to US public health, and the urgent need for appropriate policy to reduce gun-related harms, it is vital to examine the psychological and sociocultural reasons for the paradoxical attitudes of many US citizens and politicians to gun-control. US whites have twice the rate of gun ownership of blacks, oppose gun control to much greater extent than blacks, but are considerably more likely to kill themselves with those guns, than be killed by others or blacks. While the literature suggests that racism in whites shapes fear of black violence and support for policies that disadvantage blacks, no research has examined whether racism is related to gun ownership and attitudes to gun-control in US whites. This study investigated whether racism is related to gun ownership and opposition to gun control in US whites. We hypothesized that, after accounting for known confounders (i.e., age, gender, education, income, location, conservatism, political identification, anti-government sentiment), anti-black racism would be associated with having a gun in the home, and opposition to gun controls.

METHODS

The most recent data from the American National Election Study (ANES) [35] was used to test the hypothesis. The ANES panel study is the leading large-scale psychological and socio-political attitudes survey in the US, measuring various constructs and attitudes in monthly waves from a representative probability sample of US voters. Explanatory variables, including demographic details (i.e., age, gender, education, income, location: southern vs. other), anti-government sentiment, measures of conservatism (e.g., liberal versus conservative ideology), party identification (e.g., Republican versus Democrat leanings), symbolic racism, belief in a black violent stereotype, and implicit racism (i.e., race IAT), were accessed for US whites. Outcome measures were: having a gun in the home, opposition to policies banning handguns in the home, and support for permits to carry concealed handguns.

Potential participants for the ANES were contacted via telephone using random-digit-dialling and requested to complete an online survey each month from January 2008 to September 2009. Respondents were paid $10 a month for participation and those without internet access were provided with internet service for the duration of the study. The current study drew on data from several waves of the ANES survey. To counter the impact of participant drop-out and non-response on the representativeness of the sample examined in the current study we applied ANES generated weights as recommended (i.e. wave 20 post-election weight) [35]. The comprehensive ANES panel study demographics, data, materials and methods are freely available online at (http://www.electionstudies.org).

MEASURES

As part of the ANES, participants provided comprehensive information about the demographic composition of their household alongside their own background characteristics. Participants' highest level of educational attainment was grouped into five categories: less than high school diploma, high school diploma, some college but no bachelor's degree, bachelor's degree, and graduate degree. This variable was scored from 1=less than high school diploma, to 5=graduate degree. Household income in the last year was reported by all participants. Participants were instructed to include their own pre-tax income and the income of all other household members from all sources (e.g. wages, tips, interest on savings, child support, Social Security). Nineteen income bands were used ranging from 1=<$5,000 per annum to 19=≥$175,000 or more per annum. Consistent with previous research [36], education and income where dummy coded into five and four categories for analysis, respectively, rather than being treated as linear variables.

RACISM

Measures of two key types of racism against blacks were taken from the ANES for analyses: symbolic racism and implicit racial attitudes. Additionally, a single item from wave 20 of ANES was used to assess whether participants held the stereotype that blacks are violent. Participants responded to the item "How well does the word 'violent' describe most blacks?" using five response categories ranging from 1="extremely well", to 5="not at all well" (i.e. extremely well, very well, moderately well, slightly well, or not at all well). The item was coded so that a response of extremely well or very well, indicated endorsement of the black violent stereotype (coded 1), with other responses coded as 0, did not endorse stereotype blacks are violent.

In wave 20 of the ANES, participants were asked to respond to a four-item scale drawn from the Symbolic Racism Scale [37]. Specifically, participants indicated the extent to which they agree (1=agree strongly to 5=disagree strongly) with statements such as "Generations of slavery and discrimination have created conditions that make it difficult for blacks to work their way out of the lower class" (reverse scored). Scores on the four items were coded so that high scores are indicative of elevated levels of symbolic racism. A test of the reliability of the scale showed the four items corresponded closely with each other as indicated by a Cronbach's alpha level of 0.8 and the emergence of a single factor from exploratory factor analysis of the scale. We utilized the average score across the four items to produce a scale ranging 1=lowest symbolic racism score, to 5=highest symbolic racism score.

The Implicit Association Test (IAT) is commonly used in experimental psychology to gauge implicit bias. A brief race (anti-black) IAT was included in wave 19 of the ANES to assess the extent to which participants demonstrated black-white racial bias. The theoretical background, instructions, and methodology for the race IAT have been well described elsewhere [21, 22]. Briefly, the race IAT was administered online, requiring participants to rapidly associate pictures of white and black faces with positively- and negatively-valenced words. Participants were asked to press the key "P" for white faces and for positive words and "Q" for any other stimulus. Alternatively, they were asked to press "P" for black faces or positive words and "Q" for other stimuli. The test consisted of 84 stimuli, two practice runs (14 sets of stimuli each) and two data collection blocks (28 sets of stimuli each). Response latencies across blocks were analysed to produce an effect size coefficient or D score. This score is coded so that positive scores indicate an unconscious preference for whites over blacks.

CONSERVATISM, ANTI-GOVERNMENT SENTIMENT, AND POLITICAL PARTY IDENTIFICATION

Conservatism (ideological self-placement) was derived from four items assessing self-descriptions of liberal versus conservative leanings, and strength thereof. The four items were asked in wave 11 of the ANES. Participants were firstly asked "When it comes to politics, would you describe yourself as liberal, conservative, or neither liberal nor conservative?". The extent to which participants considered themselves to be liberal or conservative was then gauged with a further question: "Would you call yourself very liberal or somewhat liberal? Would you call yourself very conservative or somewhat conservative?". Those who rated themselves as "neither liberal nor conservative" were requested to indicate: "Do you think of yourself as closer to liberals, or conservatives, or neither of these?". We combined all ratings on these four items to produce a score ranging from 1 to 7 (1=extremely liberal, 4=moderate, 7=extremely conservative).

To better capture conservative values and associated views regarding government infringement on personal rights, we included a measure of anti-government sentiment. Participants responded with either a yes, immediate threat; or no, does not (yes responses coded as 1, no as 0) to the item 'Do you think the federal government has become so large and powerful that it poses an immediate threat to the rights and freedoms of ordinary citizens, or not?'.

Party identification, and the strength of this identification, was derived (wave 19) from the same process using four component questions assessing whether participants identified themselves as Republicans, Democrats, or Independents. This process yielded a score ranging from 1 to 7 (1=strong Democrat, 4=independent, 7=strong Republican).

GUN OWNERSHIP

Questions relating to household gun ownership were included in wave 19 of ANES. Participants were firstly asked if any person in the household owned any type of gun. Specifically, participants were asked: "Do you or does any other member of your household own a handgun, rifle, shotgun, or any other kind of firearm, or does no one in your household own a firearm?". Subsequently, participants were asked: "Do you happen to have in your home or garage any guns or revolvers?". This second question functioned largely to corroborate responses to the initial question, but also established the participant's personal ownership of the reported gun in the home. For analyses, a yes response to either item was coded as a 1, no responses were coded as 0.

OPINIONS ON GUN CONTROL

Participants were asked two questions regarding their views on two potential gun control policies in wave 13 of the ANES panel study. Participants were firstly asked: "Do you favor, oppose, or neither favor nor oppose making it illegal for anyone to keep a handgun at home?". Next they were asked: "Do you favor, oppose, or neither favor nor oppose giving permits to allow any adult to carry a concealed handgun if they have never been convicted of committing a crime and they have passed a test showing that they know how to use the gun safely?". To produce a clear index of whether the participant is opposed to gun control, we coded responses to the first question so that 1=definite opposition to making it illegal to keep a handgun at home, and 0=other responses. The item assessing support for a permit to carry a concealed handgun was reverse coded, so that "favor" for permits to have concealed handguns was coded as 1, which in effect represents opposition to gun control. Other responses were coded as 0, indicating non-support for concealed handguns. [...]

RESULTS

Just over half (52%) of the sample had a gun in the home, 66% opposed bans on handguns in the home, and 52% reported support for permits to carry a concealed handgun. Participants reported being slightly more conservative than liberal, and more Republican than Democratic leaning. Mean scores for symbolic racism, and to a lesser extent the race IAT, indicated anti-black sentiment; however, participants had mean scores considerably below the midpoint of scoring for the stereotype that 'blacks are violent'. Table 5 displays full weighted descriptives. [*Editor's note: Tables are not included in this text, but can be viewed online.*]

After adjusting for all explanatory variables in the model, symbolic racism was significantly related to having a gun in the home. Specifically, for each 1 point increase in symbolic racism, there was a 50% greater odds of having a gun in the home (see Table 1), and there was a 28% increase in the odds of supporting permits to carry concealed handguns (see Table 3). The relationship between symbolic racism and opposing a ban on guns in the home (27% increase in odds), was reduced (17% increase in odds) and became non-significant when the outcome 'having a gun in the home' was entered in the model (see Table 2). This is unsurprising as, in effect, opposition to gun control policy is conflated with having a gun already, and reflects self-interest [38]. Thus the gun ownership variable mediated the relationship between symbolic racism and opposition to a ban on handguns in the home. It is noteworthy that symbolic racism still main-tained its significant relationship with support for permits to carry concealed handguns in the presence of having a gun in the home.

Conservative ideology was also significantly related to stronger support for permits to carry concealed handguns after adjusting for other explanatory variables. Similarly, stronger republican identification, being from a southern state, and anti-government sentiment were associated with opposition to gun-control policies, but not with having a gun in the home. With the exception of sex, and to a much lesser extent education, demographic variables were not related to having a gun in the home or opposition to gun controls. Although sex was unrelated to having a gun in the home, there were greater odds of males being opposed to banning handguns in the home, and being supportive of permits to carry concealed handguns, than for females. This result is consistent with other US data showing that white males display the most opposition to gun control, and greater support for liberalisation of gun laws [3]. Higher education levels were associated with lower odds of having a gun in the home, but not with the gun control outcomes. This finding mirrors national data on gun ownership and support for gun control policies [3], which also shows a poor and mixed relationship between income and age, and gun ownership.

In correlation analyses, greater race IAT scores were weakly associated with greater symbolic racism scores, and with the black violent stereotype. Higher IAT scores were not related to gun ownership and gun control in full models. Higher scores on black violent stereotyping were not related to any of the gun-related outcomes; the univariate relationship between black violent stereotyping and greater support for concealed handgun permits was explained by other variables.

DISCUSSION

Opposition to gun control in US whites is somewhat paradoxical given the statistics on gun-related deaths, and such opposition may be undermining the public health of all US citizens. This study examined for the first time whether racism is related to gun ownership and the opposition to gun control in US whites. The results support the hypothesis by showing that greater symbolic racism is related to increased odds of having a gun in the home and greater opposition to gun control, after accounting for all other explanatory variables.

It is particularly noteworthy that the relationship between symbolic racism and the gun-related outcomes was maintained in the presence of conservative ideologies, political affiliation, opposition to government control, and being from a southern state, which are otherwise strong predictors of gun ownership and opposition to gun reform. Contrary to research showing associations between implicit racism and policy decision making [23], we did not find implicit racism to be significantly related to gun related outcomes after accounting for other variables. Similarly, the small correlations between the stereotype that most blacks being violent and gun outcomes were not significant after accounting for all other variables.

There are several possible reasons for the absence of multivariate associations between the stereotype of blacks as violent and race-IAT, and gun outcomes. There is considerable debate in the field regards the validity and predictive qualities of implicit measures with critical reviews and reanalyses showing weak or no association between implicit and explicit measures, and outcomes [39, 40]. Others demonstrate that non-attitudinal factors, such as, stimuli familiarity, cognitive ability, and fear of appearing racist also account for individual differences in IAT scores, that may in turn affect associations with outcome variables [39–43]. The implicit association test is also a conceptually difficult task for some to learn, and particularly the brief race-IAT used in the ANES which restricts training on this computerized measure [41]. Given the mean *D* score for the ANES race-IAT (.17) is more than twice as small as from any other studies, including one in medical doctors [44], it is also possible that participants may not have completed this complex computerized task correctly. Other authors have noted this problem with the ANES race-IAT data [45].

There are two plausible reasons for the blacks as violent stereotype not accounting for significant variance in multivariate models. First, the stereotype appears to be subsumed by symbolic racism. Table 4 shows that the black violent stereotype has its strongest relationship with symbolic racism (r=.24), and only weak relationships with other variables (rs=.06–.09). Thus, the association between the black violent stereotype and gun outcomes may be explained through its association with symbolic racism which captures negative affect towards blacks (e.g., fear, unease, hostility). Alternatively, because the black violent stereotype is a quite blatant measure, participants may have been reluctant to endorse a clearly negative view of blacks in order to avoid appearing racist. In support of this notion, only 10% of participants strongly endorsed the statement that most blacks could be described as violent, with a mean score of 2.2 on the 5-point scale, compared to a mean score of 3.5 for symbolic racism on a 5-point scale.

There are potential limitations that should be noted. The item assessing having a gun in the home does not establish that the respondent is the owner or user of that gun. This observation is born out in the absence of a sex difference to this question. Males typically have a higher rate of gun ownership than females [3]. Similarly, the gun control policy items do not assess opposition/support for assault weapons, which has been a particular focus of attention during recent gun debates in the US. Nonetheless, symbolic racism might also, quite reasonably, be related to opposition to broader gun control measures (banning assault weapons, and gun clips containing more than 10 rounds), which may or may not be effective in reducing firearms related deaths. However, although the ANES only asked participants whether there was a gun in the home, best available evidence suggests that merely having a gun in the home is associated with a marked increase in the odds of one of the members of that home dying from suicide or homicide [6, 7].

Another potential limitation is the focus on white US adults as it is possible that other US racial groups may display similar pattern of results. However, given that whites oppose gun reforms to a considerably greater extent than do blacks, or indeed any other non-white racial group, that whites are also the single largest (>70%) ethnic grouping in the US, and that symbolic racism in whites is related to numerous outcomes, the focus of the study on whites seems appropriate [3]. Indeed, in a sub-analysis of the black sample from the ANES panel study, we found that none of the variables reported in models for white participants were significantly related to any of the gun-related outcomes for blacks. Finally, the correlational nature of the study clearly prohibits causal inferences. While a view that racism underpins gun-related attitudes is plausible and supported by evidence on other race-related policy decisions [18, 23], it could be argued that there are other plausible but unmeasured variables that could explain the pattern of relationships we find here. Similarly, simply owning a firearm may lead whites to develop more negative attitudes towards blacks. There is some experimental research showing that participants who have recently held a firearm produce enhanced salivary testosterone levels and display increased aggression toward others [46]. Causality aside, greater control of firearms is the most logical direction for public health policy.

Notwithstanding these limitations, the results indicate that symbolic racism is associated with gun-related attitudes and behaviours in US whites. The statistics on firearm-related suicides and homicides in the US might reasonably be expected to convince US citizens that action on reducing gun ownership and use would be beneficial to their health. Yet, US whites oppose strong gun reform more than all other racial groups, despite a much greater likelihood that whites will kill themselves with their guns (suicide), than be killed by someone else [1]. Black-on-black homicide rates would benefit most from gun reform, and, quite logically, blacks support these reforms even if whites do not [3, 47]. Symbolic racism appears to play a role in explaining gun ownership and paradoxical attitudes to gun control in US whites. In other words, despite certain policy changes potentially benefiting whites, anti-black prejudice leads people to oppose their implementation. This finding is consistent with previous research showing that symbolic racism is associated with opposition to US policies that may benefit blacks, and support for policies that disadvantage blacks, and critically, goes beyond what is explained by other important confounders.

Gun-related deaths in the US are a significant public health concern, representing a leading cause of death, and are particularly prevalent from ages 15–54. Attitudes towards guns in many US whites appear to be influenced, like other policy preferences, by illogical racial biases. The present results suggest that gun control policies may need to be implemented independent of public opinion. The implementation of initially unpopular public health initiatives has proven effective for other public health threats (e.g., tobacco taxation, bans on smoking in public places, seatbelt use) that initially did not have widespread public and political support, but have eventually proven popular and have led to changes in attitudes [48, 49].

There remains considerable resistance in the US to even cursory gun controls, and the reasons for owning a gun and opposing gun reform (i.e., self-protection, safety, fear of crime) [4, 5], are not supported by the evidence on gun-related harms. Clearly, other motives and attitudes must be driving such paradoxical views on guns. Future research needs to examine other less obvious, yet influential, sociocultural and psychological influences on gun ownership and control, as this evidence is sparse. Evidence on the psychological and sociocultural drivers of gun ownership and resistance to strong controls will in turn help inform educational campaigns (e.g., social marketing) that may aid public acceptance of appropriate policies in the interest of the US public's health, and/or allow policy makers to implement good public health policy. The reinstatement of funding for research on gun control in the US should assist in these research endeavours.

1. What do you think about the results of this academic study? Should the results be used to reform gun control laws? How?

CHAPTER 2

WHAT THE LAWMAKERS AND POLITICIANS SAY

Although mass shootings, including Howard Unruh's infamous "Walk of Death" killing spree, have occurred in America as early as 1949, the 1999 Columbine High School massacre in Colorado arguably crystallized the mass shooting as a distinct phenomenon in the American psyche. This gave a newfound voice and urgency to those seeking gun reforms at the state and national levels.

Since then, similar incidents have occurred with disturbing regularity. In 2012, Adam Lanza entered Sandy Hook Elementary in Newtown, Connecticut, and took twenty-six lives. An aggrieved nation again wondered what could be done to prevent such an atrocity, and President Obama shed tears during a televised conference. Even more mass shootings such as the heinous attack carried out by Dylan Roof in a South Carolina church followed.

Perhaps most distressing, this uptick in mass shootings was concurrent with the expiration of previous gun control measures such as the 1994 ban on assault weapons. Meanwhile, the National Rifle Association, whose solution to gun violence is always "more guns," dug its heels in against any new gun laws.

Currently, a broad public mandate to tighten our gun laws exists, but the bipartisan support needed to pass even modest efforts such as the Manchin-Toomey bill has yet to materialize. Moreover, gun advocates argue that no law can prevent those who want a gun from obtaining one, and exploit these doubts to maintain inertia. Are lawmakers truly powerless to prevent guns from legally entering the wrong hands?

"DEMOCRAT-CONTROLLED SENATE FAILS TO PASS EVEN 'WATERED-DOWN, OVER-COMPROMISED' GUN LEGISLATION," BY JON QUEALLY, FROM *COMMON DREAMS*, APRIL 17, 2013

By a vote of 54 to 46 and as expected, the US Senate failed to pass a gun safety bill on Wednesday.

The final vote showed five Democrats voting against it and only four Republican senators voting in supported. As the *The Hill* reports, the proposed law

> would have expanded checks to cover all firearms sales at gun shows and over the Internet but would have exempted sales between friends and acquaintances outside of commercial venues.

Democrats felt confident the compromise could pass once Toomey, a Republican with an A rating from the National Rifle Association, signed on. They were caught off guard by the vigorous lobbying campaign waged by the NRA, which warned lawmakers that Manchin-Toomey would be factored in its congressional scorecard.

What appeared to be a likely victory for Obama was resoundingly defeated by the Senate as jittery Democrats facing tough re-elections next year joined nearly the entire Republican conference.

EARLIER: Despite grand promises in the wake of the Sandy Hook massacre, which left a classroom full of child victims, the gun safety legislation currently in the US Senate—already described as both 'watered-down' and 'over-compromised'—appears to be on the verge of complete defeat.

"We will not get the votes today," Sen. Joe Manchin (D-W.Va.), admitted to *NBC News* Wednesday morning.

Manchin and Sen. Pat Toomey (R-PA) were the co-sponsors of the bill that would have required an expansion of the federal background check system.

As *The Hill* reports:

[The two senators] crafted a bipartisan compromise to expand background checks to gun shows and online sales, but the measure is struggling to find the 60 votes needed in the face of gun lobby opposition.

Toomey echoed Manchin's statement Wednesday morning.

"As we sit here this morning, we don't have the votes," Toomey told National Review.

"Now, there are enough undecided people that it's still possible, but I'll be the first to admit that there is a very, very narrow path to get to 60 votes," Toomey said.

Earlier this week, *The Washington Post's* Ezra Klein characterized the legislation as weak, calling it "watered-down, over-compromised, possibly ineffective."

"This bill is already on the bubble of being too weak to really be worth it," he added.

Whether this development says more about the weakness of the US Senate, or the strength of the nation's gun lobbyists—with the NRA the supreme example—remains open to debate.

Mother Jones' Kevin Drum was blunt in his Wednesday headline: Gun Control Bill Is Dead.

Drum writes:

Keep in mind that this was (a) a very watered-down proposal, and (b) included a whole slew of goodies for gun owners. And it still couldn't get 60 votes. And while its failure is obviously partly the fault of the filibuster rule, any bill that can only get about 55 votes in the Senate never had any chance in the House anyway.

How did this happen even though, as liberals remind us endlessly, 90 percent of the American public supports background checks? Because about 80 percent of those Americans think it sounds like a reasonable idea but don't really care much. I doubt that one single senator will suffer at the polls in 2014 for voting against Manchin-Toomey.

Gun control proposals poll decently all the time. But the plain truth is that there are only a small number of people who feel really strongly about it, and they mostly live in urban blue districts already. Outside of that, pro-gun control opinion is about an inch deep. This is a classic case where poll literalism leads you completely astray. Without measuring intensity of feeling, that 90 percent number is meaningless.

1. Would the Manchin-Toomey Amendment do enough to close private gun sale loopholes, in your opinion?

2. As of now, this moderate legislation proposal is dead. What do you see as the chances of a revived bill getting through Congress?

"CITIES FIND NEW WAYS TO GO AFTER GUN VIOLENCE," BY J.B. WOGAN, FROM *GOVERNING*, SEPTEMBER 2014

In January 2013, one month after the school massacre at Newtown, Conn., Philadelphia Mayor Michael Nutter stood in a U.S. Senate briefing room, next to a display of semi-automatic rifles, and delivered a reminder to the reporters and gun control advocates gathered around him. "Too many times in the last few years," Nutter said, "mayors have expressed shock at mass shootings. Even more frequently, many of us must cope with gun violence that occurs on the streets of our cities day after day after day after day."

Nutter was there to promote federal firearms legislation, including an assault rifle ban and a requirement that gun dealers conduct background checks to screen out criminals and mentally disturbed purchasers. But as he pointed out, most of the roughly 11,000 gun homicides in America in a given year aren't mass killings perpetrated by deranged people using military-grade weapons. They usually involve only a few people at a time, often the product of gang feuding, personal quarrels or domestic disputes, carried out with ordinary handguns, not semi-automatic rifles. And even though gun murders have declined everywhere in recent years, the rates remain much higher in the urban cores of large metro areas.

The campaign for federal legislation died on the Senate floor that spring, and only a handful of states imposed major new limits on guns thereafter. That limited success by gun control advocates underscored a truth that Nutter and mayors all over the country understand perfectly well: Reducing the amount of gun violence in this country is now essentially a local issue, one that city leaders have to pursue on their home ground. But they have to pursue it carefully, avoiding outright bans on the possession or carrying of weapons. As a series of court decisions at various levels has made clear in the past few years, anything close to an outright gun ban is not going to survive judicial scrutiny.

In enacting new laws against gun violence, mayors and other civic leaders are challenging not only the courts but the strong pro-gun sentiment that exists in most state legislatures. In the past decade, Philadelphia alone has seen courts invalidate about a half-dozen local gun laws, including two bans on semi-automatic rifles, limits on the frequency of handgun purchases (one a month) and a requirement that gun owners be licensed before bringing a firearm into the city. Pennsylvania courts have held that only the legislature can pass laws pertaining to buying and owning a gun--and the legislature has shown no interest in doing so.

As a result, anti-violence activists in Philadelphia and other cities in the country have had to get more creative in their push to reduce the number of guns on the streets. The approaches vary widely, from punishing reckless behavior by gun owners to rewarding businesses that take voluntary steps to prevent violent criminals from acquiring guns. What these approaches have in common, though, is a shift away from going after weapons themselves to a new focus on curtailing their unsafe use.

In Sunnyvale, Calif., for example, voters approved a measure designed to discourage straw gun purchases, in which one person buys a gun for someone else, by imposing reporting requirements on gun owners when their firearms are lost or stolen. Travis, Texas, decided to require that the only gun show in town make criminal background checks mandatory for all firearms sales. Dallas announced a new program--already supported by state law, but not enforced--that temporarily confiscates firearms from people on probation for domestic violence. And in Tucson, Ariz., the city council passed an ordinance that empowers police to request alcohol testing of anyone they suspect fired a gun while intoxicated.

The Tucson ordinance may invite legal challenges because Arizona has a state law preempting local measures against buying or owning guns. But that's a debate welcomed by Councilman Steve Kozachik, sponsor of the alcohol-testing bill and another bill on reporting lost or stolen firearms. The state might have free rein on laws about purchase and ownership, he says, but the city ought to have some say on illegal and unsafe behavior. "If someone steals your gun, call the police. If you're drunk, don't use your weapon," he says. "This is not anti-Second Amendment."

While Tucson targets the behavior of gun owners, cities elsewhere want to change the behavior of gun businesses. Last year, the U.S. Conference of Mayors published a code of conduct for companies in municipal pension investment portfolios. Similarly, Philadelphia had about $15 million invested in businesses that sell guns and ammunition, including Smith and Wesson, Walmart and Sears. Its pension board required that those companies agree to conduct criminal background checks for all gun transactions and to ensure that their business partners--mostly gun shows and gun dealers--abide by the same stringent standard.

Two other public pension boards in Philadelphia adopted the same code of conduct for pension investing, and later last year mayors in Los Angeles and Chicago announced that they, too, would try to leverage their pension funds to force a change in the gun industry, focusing attention on gun manufacturers that still sold high-capacity magazines and semi-automatic rifles after mass shootings in 2012. Though the pension idea gained traction around the country, it may not yield the intended result. Last September, more than a dozen affected companies in Philadelphia's portfolio refused to adopt the city's gun principles, prompting its pension board to divest in all of them.

Nonetheless, the marketplace is an increasingly attractive arena for cities to apply gun policy without resorting to regulation. In January, Jersey City, N. J., Mayor Steven Fulop capitalized on his city police department's need to buy roughly $350,000 in firearms and ammunition as a way to influence gun suppliers. To bid on the city police contract, the companies had to explain what they do with old weapons and how they comply with federal and state background check laws. As with local ordinances on lost or stolen firearms, Jersey City's questions were meant to encourage the private sector to clamp down voluntarily on illegal and straw purchases, both of which are ways that criminals acquire guns.

Fulop wants the market-based approach to have ramifications beyond his own city, which is why he's recruiting other mayors to ask the same questions. Nutter in Philadelphia and Seattle Mayor Ed Murray both say they may incorporate similar questions in their departments' next big gun purchase. "We've got to build scale," Fulop says. "The goal is by the end of this year to have enough cities involved that we could actually impact the dialogue through our pricing."

Separate from Fulop's efforts, 20 cities in Florida have formed a coalition that plans to impose new disclosure requirements in their bidding process for police contracts. Led by the nonprofit Arms with Ethics, the municipalities have committed to asking whether manufacturers run criminal background checks on their employees and what they do when they discover a retailer has been implicated in a gun crime. Members of the coalition can choose from a menu of suggested questions, but some say they'll ask if gun businesses train their employees to identify straw purchasers so that they can avoid selling guns likely to end up at a crime scene. Others want to know if gun dealers maintain quarterly and annual inventories to see if any firearms are missing--something that the U.S. Bureau of Alcohol, Tobacco, Firearms and Explosives can't legally require. Taken together, says Casey Woods, the executive director of Arms with Ethics, the questions encourage "things that people think are already law, but aren't."

The market-based approach is too new to evaluate for impact, but critics question whether city police departments represent enough market share to change industry practices. Gun purchases by city police represent a small fraction of overall gun sales in a given year--roughly 15 percent, according to IBISWorld, a market-research firm. Then again, police are disproportionately influential gun consumers, argues Gregory Gundlach, a marketing professor at the University of North Florida who first outlined the Jersey City-style approach in 2010. "The purchases are made in a static sense, but they're also reoccurring," Gundlach says. "Manufacturers realize that the lifetime economic value of law enforcement is pretty high because these sales aggregate over time." Also, he adds, the guns that police choose to buy have spillover effects on the civilian market because average citizens often imitate police in their purchasing decisions.

Shortly after gun legislation stalled in Congress last year, a spate of local homicides prompted the city council in Richmond, Calif., to consider new municipal regulations. As recently as 2008, Richmond ranked as one of the nation's 10 most violent cities of more than 100,000 residents. Almost all its homicides and half of its robberies involved guns. Nonetheless, Councilman Tom Butt, a self-described champion of gun control, voted against a resolution that would have studied options for new gun regulation. California already has some of the strictest gun laws in the country, he says, but "it's not enough. Regardless of what kind of gun laws you have, people who really want to have a gun are going to find one."

Seven years ago, Butt became an early supporter of a local antiviolence strategy that sidesteps guns entirely and focuses instead on the people who use them. "Illegal guns have always found their way into urban communities by some mechanism," says DeVone Boggan, the director of neighborhood safety in the Richmond mayor's office. "We need to find a way to get these young men not to pick these guns up, to develop the mindset that 'I'm not going to deal with conflict by using a gun.'"

With the help of a data analyst from the police department and tips from street informants, Boggan's office identifies young men who are suspected of being involved in a shooting--but who have not been charged or convicted--and invites them to join the city's peace fellowship program. The perks of being a peace fellow include trips outside the city or even outside the country (destinations have included Cape Town and Dubai), plus financial rewards for participating longer than six months. While those benefits help recruit program participants, the real boon is the support services available to the city's peace fellows. A team of older neighborhood residents --often with a criminal past--coaches the men on setting goals and mapping out the small, specific steps needed to accomplish everything from obtaining a driver's license to applying for college. A caretaker accompanies the fellows through the maze of social services that they may need to stabilize their lives, from housing to drug addiction counseling. Finally, every fellow takes classes on anger management.

Boggan's holistic approach to gun violence started in 2007. As of this past July, the program had recruited 68 peace fellows, with 25 completing the full 15 months. Fifty-seven had avoided being charged with a firearm assault since joining. All but three were still alive. The public image of the peace fellowship received a boost in January when the police department reported that 2013 saw the lowest number of annual homicides in three decades.

Since the program's launch, other cities in California and around the country have called Boggan for advice on how to introduce a peace fellowship in their own jurisdictions. Public safety officials express excitement about the approach, he says, but by the end of the discussion they're pessimistic about replicating the fellowship. "The challenge," Boggan says, "is being able to go back home and sell this idea of providing positive resources to individuals who have often committed heinous crimes."

Indeed, it's an open question whether other cities will want to use a Richmond-style program as a road map for tackling gun violence. One of the model's biggest assets, says Angela Wolf, a community psychologist studying the program, is long-term intensive mentoring that extends beyond the fellows' graduation. At least two years later, former fellows still call their mentors for advice about how to handle a conflict or career decision. The model requires a major investment of time and money to turn around the lives of a small number of residents. Nonetheless, Boggan argues that supporting a few violent residents with human resources might be the most efficient use of tax dollars. When the city hired Boggan in 2007, it faced a $24 million structural deficit, much of it driven by expenditures of $6 million per year for law enforcement. Like most cities, Richmond had responded to spikes in violent crime by hiring more officers and putting violent people in jail. That was expensive, and it wasn't doing much to solve the problem. "If you look at most cities where the public safety budget is going through the roof, it's justified by the actions of a relatively small group of men doing a lot of damage," Boggan says. "We have to identify alternative solutions that are much more responsive."

1. How would you expect conflicts between local and federal gun legislation to play out? Do you think municipal efforts will be invalidated by the Second Amendment, or do you think the Supreme Court will allow such experiments?

2. Do you support the type of personalized rehabilitation for shooting suspects described above?

"EIGHT STATES HAVE PASSED LAWS VOIDING FEDERAL FIREARMS REGULATIONS," BY JUSTINE MCDANIEL, ROBBY KORTH, AND JESSICA BOEHM, FROM *NEWS21*, AUGUST 16, 2014

Across the country, a thriving dissatisfaction with the U.S. government is prompting a growing spate of bills in state legislatures aimed at defying federal control over firearms - more than 200 during the last decade, a News21 investigation found.

Particularly in Western and Southern states, where individual liberty intersects with increasing skepticism among gun owners, firearms are a political vehicle in efforts to ensure states' rights and void U.S. gun laws within their borders. State legislators are attempting to declare that only they have the right to interpret the Second Amendment, a movement that recalls the anti-federal spirit of the Civil War and civil-rights eras.

"I think the president and the majority of Congress, both in the House and Senate, are just completely out of touch with how people feel about Second Amendment rights," said Missouri state Sen. Brian Nieves, who has fought for bills to weaken the federal government's authority over firearms in his state.

In Idaho, the Legislature unanimously passed a law to keep any future federal gun measures from being enforced in the state. In Kansas, a law passed last year says federal regulation doesn't apply to guns manufactured in the state. Wyoming, South Dakota and Arizona have had laws protecting "firearms freedom" from the U.S. government since 2010.

A News21 analysis shows 14 such bills were passed by legislators in 11 states, mainly in Western states, along with Kansas, Tennessee and Alaska. Of those, 11 were signed into law, though one was later struck down in court. In Montana, Missouri and Oklahoma, three others were vetoed.

More than three-quarters of U.S. states have proposed nullification laws since 2008. More than half of those bills have come in the last two years after the shooting at Sandy Hook Elementary School in Newtown, Connecticut. All but three have been introduced since President Barack Obama took office.

Underneath the policy jargon lies a culture of firearms woven into the heritage and politics of states whose histories were shaped by guns.

"(The federal government) is diving off into areas unchecked that they're not supposed to be involved in," said Montana state Rep. Krayton Kerns, who introduced a bill in 2013 to limit the ability of local police to help enforce federal laws. "Not only is it our right in state legislatures to do this, it's our obligation to do it. Somebody's got to put a 'whoa' on it."

Opponents say it's not federal gun regulation that's unconstitutional, but laws to nullify it.

The Brady Center to Prevent Gun Violence filed a lawsuit against Kansas on July 9 to stop enforcement of the state's recently passed Second Amendment Protection Act.

"The law should not be called the Second Amendment Protection Act, it should be called the Gun Violence

Preservation Act," said Jonathan Lowy, director of the center's Legal Action Project.

Two types of bills are the primary vehicles for the movement, both based on model legislation introduced in statehouses from Tallahassee to Juneau.

The first type holds that federal laws do not apply to firearms manufactured and sold within a given state, relying on the Constitution's interstate commerce clause. It says Congress can regulate trade between states, but says nothing about trade within states.

Under Utah law, for example, guns made, purchased and used in the state are exempt from federal laws. Commonly known as the Firearms Freedom Act, versions of the law have been debated during 78 legislative sessions across 37 states in the last decade.

The other approach says gun regulation falls outside the scope of the federal government's power, making it state territory. Such bills, often known as the Second Amendment Preservation Act, usually say state officials cannot enforce federal gun laws or limit the ability to do so, and some bills have tried to impose penalties on officers who help federal officials.

"It's basically saying, 'Federal government, if you want to enforce federal firearms laws in the state of Arizona, you're welcome to do it, but we won't give you any assistance. So in other words, no state police help with (Bureau of Alcohol, Tobacco, Firearms and Explosives) raids, no local law enforcement enforcing a federal gun law, none of that," said Mike Maharrey, national communications director of the Tenth Amendment Center, a for-profit nullification group based in California.

The Kansas law makes it a felony for federal officials to enforce U.S. firearm law.

The Brady Center suit against the Sunflower State indicates that some are beginning to view nullification as a threat.

"This is a matter both of constitutional law and common sense," said Stuart Plunkett, a Brady Center attorney in that case. "Our system of laws would break down if each of the 50 states could offer its own interpretation of congressional authority over interstate commerce."

But the bill's sponsor and co-author, Republican Rep. John Rubin, said he believes it's the Brady Center that errs in interpretation of government authority regarding intrastate commerce. Rubin, who spent much of his professional career as a government lawyer and in administrative law thinks U.S. government overreach is the problem.

"The founders never envisioned ... that a modern federal government would construe the commerce clause so broadly as to enable the federal government to regulate every aspect of the lives of the states," Rubin said.

The Tenth Amendment Center responded to the Brady Center suit with a pledge to ramp up its campaign to pass Second Amendment Preservation Acts in more states in 2015.

"To us, this is a BIG green light to push harder than ever to protect the 2nd Amendment through state level resistance to federal gun-control measures," Tenth Amendment Center founder Michael Boldin wrote in a July 9 statement.

In Kentucky, Rep. Diane St. Onge has already introduced a nullification bill for the 2015 session.

Although she's sure a court challenge will come from the federal government if the bill is passed, she believes it will hold up.

"We're making a statement here about what we hold true, what we believe in here in Kentucky," St. Onge said.

The federal government has said little on the matter, but U.S. Attorney General Eric Holder rebuked Kansas for its law in April.

"In purporting to override federal law and to criminalize the official acts of federal officers, (Kansas' law) directly conflicts with federal law and is therefore unconstitutional," Holder wrote in a letter to Kansas Gov. Sam Brownback.

The measures often fizzle, even in conservative states. The National Rifle Association doesn't support nullifying federal gun laws because that could undo NRA legislative success in Washington.

"I think that is a misguided distraction," said Todd Rathner, an NRA board member from Arizona. "I empathize with what they're trying to accomplish, but I am not convinced it's the right way to do it."

In Montana, where the largely rural population is spread out over nearly 150,000 square miles of mountains, fields and valleys, one man has been pushing these bills since 2005.

Gary Marbut, president of the Montana Shooting Sports Association, has written scores of gun bills that have been introduced since 1985 in the Montana statehouse, 64 of which have become law.

Marbut lives on his family's old ranch, in a secluded geodesic dome near Missoula. A self-appointed guardian of state gun rights, he has failed in three bids for a seat in the Montana Legislature, but succeeded in starting a movement to weaken federal authority of guns across the country.

Marbut, who is running for state representative in 2014, didn't expect other states to take up the cause. When it comes to the gun bills that challenge federal law, Marbut's focus on guns seems almost incidental. His true target is challenging federal authority.

"I would like to see some of this power shifted back from governments, especially the federal government, to the states and to the people," Marbut said in his home on an overcast morning in June.

This view appears to be shared by Montanans. The pioneer spirit that brought their ancestors to the West still runs throughout Montana and neighboring states. That independence, locals say, is what influences their views on guns.

"There is kind of a 'leave me alone to live my life' attitude in the state," said Jim Smith, mayor of Helena, the state capital. "There's only a million of us here and there's vast acreage, six people per square mile."

For Democrats and Republicans alike, guns are part of a time-honored and highly practical way of life.

Gun use is tied to family traditions: Firearm skills are passed down from parent to child. Elk hunts are social gatherings, gun safety is taught to 11-year-olds.

It was here that the first Firearm Freedoms Act, written by Marbut, was introduced. After three attempts in the Legislature, it passed in 2009. Its spark lit a nationwide fervor among those who want the federal government to get out of their lives.

"I designed it as a way to test federal commerce-clause power using firearms as the vehicle for the exercise," Marbut said. The law said that guns made in Montana are not subject to federal law.

Almost immediately after its passage, Marbut announced he would manufacture a Montana-made rifle, but he was challenged by the Bureau of Alcohol, Tobacco, Firearms and Explosives, so he sued for his right to make the guns.

Eventually, the suit made it to the 9th U.S. Circuit Court of Appeals, which ruled against Marbut. He tried to take the case to the Supreme Court, but it declined to hear the case earlier this year.

This libertarian streak, coupled with a deep-seated appreciation of the Second Amendment, is at the heart of the expanding national movement to nullify federal law.

"We could be arguing over crescent wrenches if they wanted to make that the debate," said Kerns, the state representative from Laurel, Montana.

"It just boils down to the federal government stepping across a boundary that they shouldn't."

Kansas Republican Rubin echoed Kerns' views for a bill that relies on the commerce clause and also punishes federal agents for enforcing federal law.

"To me, the Second Amendment Protection Act is even more about the Tenth Amendment than the Second Amendment," Rubin said.

One of the major forces behind these bills isn't even a gun rights group.

The Tenth Amendment Center, which created the model firearms legislation known as the Second Amendment Preservation Act, is actually focused on the Tenth

Amendment, which says any powers not granted to the federal government by the Constitution belong to the states.

The group's "Tenther movement" promotes federal firearm law nullification, but also advocates legalizing marijuana and nixing Common Core education standards.

"The kind of motto of our organization is, follow the Constitution every time, no exceptions, no excuses," Maharrey said. "So we focus on any constitutional issue and try to limit federal power to its constitutionally delegated role."

However, others say nullification efforts will not stand up in court.

Adam Winkler, a law professor at the University of California, Los Angeles, said that both types of nullification laws are unconstitutional.

"States are not entitled to nullify federal law," he said. "Any law that interferes with a valid federal law is unconstitutional. The federal law is supreme over state law."

"Nullification is no more valid today than it was during the 1950s during desegregation or during the pre-Civil War era," Brady Center attorney Plunkett said.

But constitutional conservatives aren't giving up.

Of the more than 200 bills introduced in the last decade, 130 have come in the two years since the Newtown shooting, a time of renewed advocacy for gun control legislation by Congress. With federal gun laws staying in the news and the nullification trend spreading, many gun rights advocates continue pushing to void U.S. law.

If the fight continues, it has the potential to have a broad effect on states' rights. Although nullification is a recurrent challenge to the federal government, it rarely succeeds.

What seems like a purely pro-gun trend speaks to a deeper dissatisfaction among a large swath of Americans and a desire to spurn the federal government in today's highly polarized political times.

"I think it's part of a larger interest in pushing back against federal power," said Maharrey.

"I think the gun debate's become more pronounced over the last couple of years due to some of the tragedies that we've seen, but on the other hand, interest in general of re-establishing state sovereignty and limiting federal power ... has also grown," he said.

1. It seems like recent mass shootings have catalyzed some states to make their gun laws more relaxed. Why do you think these changes would occur after such tragic events?

"TWO STATES, SAME CHALLENGE: LAWMAKERS IN COLORADO AND CONNECTICUT MADE TOUGH CALLS IN THE WAKE OF MASS SHOOTINGS," BY LYNN BARTELS, FROM *STATE LEGISLATURES*, JULY/AUGUST 2013

America's divide over gun ownership rights and regulations is not new, but rarely has the debate been so emotional. In the wake of the mass shootings in Colorado and Connecticut in 2012, state legislatures have looked at hundreds of proposals pushed by both sides: from arming schoolteachers and nullifying federal firearms restrictions, for example, to banning high-capacity weapons and holding firearms manufacturers liable for shootings.

Legislators have introduced roughly 2,356 gun bills since shortly after the Newtown, Conn., shootings in which 20 children and six adults were killed in December 2012. In April, an analysis of about 1,500 of the bills by the Sunlight Foundation, which monitors transparency in government, found them to be about evenly split between weakening or strengthening gun restrictions. Last year, only 35 percent of gun bills would have strengthened regulations, according to the Law Center to Prevent Gun Violence.

As of mid-June, approximately 202 of the 2,356 gun-related bills had become law, according to NCSL research. They run the gamut, from New York's limit of seven bullets per magazine to Arkansas' Church Protection Act, giving places of worship the authority to allow guns on their premises.

LAWMAKERS RESPOND

Lawmakers in Connecticut and Colorado were forced into addressing gun laws following the movie theater shooting that killed 12 people and injured 58 in Aurora, Colo., in July, and the tragedy at Sandy Hook Elementary School five months later.

Both states passed greater restrictions on guns, but the route each legislature took and the opposition the legislation faced varied greatly, even though both states have Democratic governors and Democratic-controlled legislatures.

Connecticut legislators made sweeping changes in a single bill that many consider one of the strictest in the nation. Among its provisions are an expanded assault weapons ban, a restriction on high-capacity magazines and registration for the purchase of ammunition and all guns.

Colorado legislators passed five new guns laws. They're tamer than Connecticut's, but for a Western state, where gun ownership is high and where guns have long been used to hunt and protect property, their passage surprised many. Colorado's new laws limit ammunition magazines to 15 rounds, institute universal background checks for the sale and transfer of weapons, and require gun buyers to pay for background checks, among other things.

Legislative chambers in both states became stages for the national debate. Hearings drew unprecedented crowds, mostly those opposed to any kind of restriction on the right to bear arms. Gun control advocates argued back with facts and figures: 85 Americans die daily from gun—53 of them suicides—a rate that far exceeds most other developed countries.

Supporters of tougher gun laws call them common-sense reforms. "They ensure that law-abiding citizens have full access to guns for all lawful purposes but that criminals do not," says Colorado Senate Majority Leader Morgan Carroll (D). "Weapons in the hands of criminals or the dangerously mentally ill hurt our communities and take away the rights of other citizens to live."

Second Amendment activists viewed the 2012 shootings as evidence the country needs more guns. Had more people been armed in Sandy Hook Elementary School or the Aurora theater, they argued, the killers likely would have been gunned down, either preventing the massacres or at least limiting the carnage. The Newtown and Aurora killers specifically chose a school and a theater because they knew the occupants would be unarmed, many argued.

"It's obvious you're safer when law-abiding people have guns," says Colorado Senator Greg Brophy (R). "Even our sheriffs said the new laws won't make anyone safer."

WHAT THE LAWS DO

Connecticut's new gun law:
- Expands the assault weapons ban
- Prohibits high-capacity magazines
- Requires background checks on all firearms sales
- Mandates registration to purchase ammunition and all guns
- Increases funding for security and mental health treatment.

Colorado's five new guns laws:
- Limit ammunition magazines to 15 rounds
- Mandate universal background checks on the sale and transfer of weapons
- Require gun buyers to pay for background checks
- Ban certain domestic violence offenders from owning guns
- Require applicants for concealed-carry permits to demonstrate their competence with a gun in the presence of a certified instructor.

COOPERATION IN CONNECTICUT

Connecticut's gun bill had strong bipartisan support, including the backing of Senate Minority Leader John McKinney (R), whose district includes Newtown, and House Minority Leader Larry Cafero (R). Leaders from both parties talked about how to respond after the Sandy Hook Elementary School shootings, says Senate President Donald E. Williams Jr. (D). "It was a remarkable moment in our legislative history in Connecticut. We were able to come together in a bipartisan way and take action on what is arguably the most divisive issue in American politics," Williams says.

Connecticut lawmakers introduced dozens of gun bills; some died on the calendar, others were merged into the 139-page bill that ultimately passed. The legislature held public meetings—including one in Newtown. The Senate vote on the prevailing bill was 26-10, with 20 of 22 Democrats and six of 14 Republicans in support. The House vote was 105-44, with 85 of 99 Democrats and 20 of 52 Republicans in support. One Democrat and one Republican were absent.

Connecticut Senator Andrew Maynard (D), one of the two Democrats opposed to the bill, says he believes emotion overcame logic. "The nature of the crime demanded some sort of action, but we took a knee-jerk approach to it." He says he's not sure the expanded weapons ban and the magazine limits will make Connecticut safer, and was upset to see "thoughtful" hunters and sportsmen who opposed more controls labeled "gun nuts."

CONTROVERSY IN COLORADO

Colorado's battle over gun laws was more partisan than Connecticut's. When Colorado Democrats unveiled their bills, they faced fierce opposition from the GOP, gun rights groups and even some members of the Democratic caucus. Republicans made clear from the beginning they didn't believe in what Colorado Senate Minority Leader Bill Cadman (R) called "meaningless, feel-good legislation."

Democrats drafted their proposals without much GOP input. The most controversial, sponsored by Senate President John Morse (D), would have held manufacturers, sellers and owners of weapons liable for deaths they caused. Morse eventually withdrew it after delivering a blistering attack on the gun lobby.

Morse, now the subject of a recall attempt over the gun bills, says it was worth it. "If making Colorado safer from gun violence costs me my political career, it is an amazingly small price to pay," he says.

Those opposed to the legislation feared it was only the beginning of an eventual total government ban on personal gun ownership. "This is step one," said Colorado Senator Brophy. A frustrated Colorado Senate Minority Leader Cadman accused supporters of the bills of being controlled by outsiders, including New York Mayor Michael Bloomberg and his group, Mayors Against Illegal Guns. He displayed a New York flag in the Senate Republican Office in protest. (New York was the first state to pass stricter gun laws following the Connecticut shootings.)

Gun ownership for many in the Rocky Mountain state is such a cherished value that after the bills passed, some rural residents even threatened to secede.

Of the five bills that became law, only the one limiting online concealed-carry training received any GOP support, with five of 43 Republicans in both chambers voting for it. Colorado Senate Majority Leader Carroll says Democrats were proud they "were able to get done what Congress couldn't get done."

After Colorado Governor John Hickenlooper (D) signed the bills, all but 10 of Colorado's 64 county sheriffs joined in a federal lawsuit seeking to block them, arguing two of the laws violate the constitutional right to bear arms. Connecticut Governor Dannel Malloy (D) is facing a similar suit.

The laws also could cost the states revenue if manufacturers of weapons and weapons accessories based in Colorado and Connecticut move to other states, as a few have threatened.

BLUE STATE, PURPLE STATE

Governors Hickenlooper and Malloy talked after their tragedies and as their legislatures geared up. "As [Malloy] described what Connecticut was considering, I would say, 'Boy, that would never fly in Colorado,'" Hickenlooper says. "They were much more aggressive than a Western state would be, but if you look at their demographics, they're a blue, blue, blue state."

In contrast, Colorado voters are almost equally divided among Republicans, Democrats and unaffiliated. "Republicans rule," read the headline in the Rocky Mountain News after the 2002 election. But only two years later, Democrats picked up a U.S. Senate seat, a U.S. House seat and control of both chambers of the legislature, a feat the party had not achieved since 1960. The state has remained purple in recent years. In 2010, the GOP knocked off two Democratic incumbents in the U.S. House and today, Republicans serve as attorney general, treasurer and secretary of state.

In Connecticut, Democrats hold every congressional seat and every statewide constitutional office. And although Connecticut is the home of the trade association for the firearms industry and several prominent gun makers, including Colt's Manufacturing, Stag Arms and Sturm, Ruger and Co., a Quinnipiac University poll taken in March showed broad support for tougher gun laws there—even among Republicans.

House Minority Leader Cafero told the Hartford Courant that a Republican presence at the negotiating table helped stop some of the stricter gun control measures Democrats initially sought, including limits on the number of guns people could own and steep taxes on ammunition. "I felt I had an obligation to make sure there was a balance between the safety of the public ... and the protection of Second Amendment and law-abiding gun owners," Cafero says.

For Colorado Representative Rhonda Fields of Aurora, passage of the gun laws was a personal victory. She lost her son and his fiancé to gun violence in 2005. Because of her activism in the case, she was appointed to a vacancy in the Colorado House of Representatives. She subsequently was elected to the seat and now represents the Aurora district where the recent theater shootings occurred. Fields sponsored three of the five gun bills that became law but says she was unprepared for the anger the legislation spawned.

"I had no idea the Capitol would be stormed ... that people would circle the Capitol for hours honking their horns." She received a series of threatening, racist emails that led to an arrest, a new home security system and state trooper presence when she is at the Capitol. Although Fields is still fearful, she says she has no regrets about the legislation.

ARMING SCHOOL PERSONNEL

In 2013, legislators in more than 30 states introduced bills authorizing K-12 school staff to carry firearms. Specifics varied widely—from calling for principals to carry concealed weapons to creating school marshal programs to train teachers, administrators and janitors in gun use. Most of the bills failed. The ones that passed make the following changes:

- In Alabama, current and retired school employees can now form volunteer emergency security forces, and districts must establish policies addressing the carrying and storing of their weapons.
- In Arkansas, a church that operates a private school may allow people with concealed-carry permits to carry guns on school property. And, colleges may allow faculty to carry guns on campus if the governing board does not have a policy prohibiting it.
- In Kansas, school districts may allow employees with concealed-carry permits to carry guns on campus if the district does not have a policy prohibiting it.
- South Dakota's "school sentinels" law authorizes districts to create, establish and supervise the arming of school employees, hired security personnel or volunteers.
- Tennessee allows certain school employees to carry a firearm on school grounds if they are licensed, meet certain qualifications, and have written authorization from authorities.
- The Protection of Texas Children Act permits schools to designate an employee as a marshal who can use a firearm to deal with potential crises.

—*Lauren Heintz and Michelle Camacho Liu*

"Doing nothing," she says, "is not an answer." But for gun rights activists, what lawmakers in Colorado and Connecticut did isn't the answer either.

© National Conference of State Legislatures

1. To gun advocates, the answer to high-profile instances of gun violence such as school shootings is often more "good guys" with guns. Is there any possible merit to this approach?

2. The stated aim of keeping guns away from criminals has surface appeal. Yet, a "criminal" would, by definition, be incarcerated. Therefore, we're actually talking about limiting the rights of former criminals with these laws. Is there any way this might be problematic or racist?

CHAPTER 3

WHAT THE COURTS SAY

"A well regulated Militia, being necessary to the security of a free State, the right of the people to keep and bear Arms, shall not be infringed." These twenty-seven words, otherwise known as the Second Amendment, have been subject to more extensive judicial scrutiny throughout the nation's history than almost any other part of the Constitution.

In two recent cases, *District of Columbia v. Heller* and *McDonald v. City of Chicago*, the courts set some parameters around the Second Amendment, but did not enumerate the specific technical limits otherwise known as "gun-control." In the former case, the Supreme Court ruled 5-4 that a ban on handguns in federal enclaves is unconstitutional. *McDonald* extended this ruling to the states. Although both decisions protect an individual's right to possess a handgun for defense, making outright bans on handguns unlawful, neither delineated an absolute right to carry these guns outside the home. Under both rulings, regulations on concealed carry, assault weapons, and background checks are all completely legal.

Staunch gun rights advocates see these cases as high-cost victories. Although the right to bear arms is now enshrined as an individual right, the Supreme Court left the specifics of gun laws up to states and municipalities. So far, the high court has not struck down any gun control measures—provided that none of these prevent law-abiding citizens from keeping guns in their homes for protection. Thus, leeway exists for stringent gun laws, provided the culture moves away from "no-compromise" rhetoric.

"EXPLAINER: WHAT IS THE 2ND AMENDMENT AND HOW DOES IT IMPACT US GUN CONTROL?," BY JONATHAN PARKER, FROM *THE CONVERSATION* WITH THE PARTNERSHIP OF KEELE UNIVERSITY, JUNE 15, 2016

The Second Amendment to the Constitution is a touchstone for the many people who identify with American society's enduring affinity for firearms. And every time there is an atrocity, such as the mass shooting in Orlando, debate inevitably settles on how this part of the Constitution effectively prevents the adoption of workable gun control measures.

But ironically, the Amendment played almost no substantial part in legal or constitutional jurisprudence involving gun ownership until 2008 and even the recent change in Supreme Court interpretations does not give it a significant role in gun regulation. The importance of the Second Amendment lies much more in its symbolism for those people defending gun ownership and as a rallying point for those supporters.

The Amendment is a telling reminder of America's longstanding relationship with guns that goes back to its colonial heritage and has developed a strong and popular mythology surrounding this legacy. But it is not a clear endorsement of the right to own a gun. The text reads:

> *A well regulated Militia, being necessary to the security of a free State, the right of the people to keep and bear Arms, shall not be infringed.*

The Amendment came out of the colonies' longstanding suspicion of standing armies, accentuated by the recent War of Independence against Great Britain. It sought to enshrine protections for local and state militias, who would provide a bulwark against any possible encroachment of power by the new national government – and its national army – which was established by the Constitution in 1789.

The Second Amendment was always about federalism, protecting the power of the states to have and regulate militias rather than granting individual rights, and the courts interpreted it that way consistently until two cases in 2008 and 2010 completely upended more than two centuries of legal and constitutional history.

LEGAL FRONTIERS

In the case of District of Columbia v. Heller, 554 U.S. 570 (2008), the Supreme Court held that the Second Amendment protects an individual right to possess a firearm – independent of any service in a militia – for legal purposes such as self-defence. In a subsequent case, McDonald v. Chicago, 561 U.S. 3025 (2010), the Court extended this protection against bans by all state and local governments.

These cases established the individual right to gun ownership for the first time – but, significantly, they were only applied in relation to absolute bans. The Supreme Court continues to allow almost all restrictions on firearms short of an outright ban. It is the politics of gun regulation that is much more important if you want to understand the gun debate in the US. The Second Amendment, meanwhile, is a political symbol rather than a strong legal protection.

DECLINING OWNERSHIP AND HOMICIDES

An understanding of the place of guns in American culture is needed to fully understand the issue of gun regulation. The General Social Survey (GSS), has found that gun ownership has declined from 49% of households in 1973 to 34% in 2010, though Gallup opinion polls report a lower figure, unchanged from 1972 to 2010 at 43%. Whichever figure is most accurate, a substantial portion of American households own a gun. Traditionally, hunting was the main purpose for gun ownership but it has declined from 49% in 1999 to 32% in 2013. Personal protection has now become the main reason cited by gun owners, rising from 26% in 1999 to 48% in 2013.

Despite worries over personal safety, fueled by widespread media coverage of regular mass shootings, the homicide rate from firearms has fallen hugely in the US since the 1990s. Compared with 1993, the peak of US gun homicides, the firearm homicide rate was 49% lower in 2010. The rate for other violent crimes with a firearm was 75% lower in 2011 than in 1993. While violent crime has plummeted since the 1990s, however, mass shootings consume most efforts around gun control today. People believe that crime has gone up rather than down – and this continuing fear of crime influences gun policy.

OPINION POLARIZED

Public opinion has been decidedly in favour of stricter gun control for decades, but the recent polarisation of politics in the US has also influenced people's views on guns. Support for gun control is now roughly matched with support for gun rights in the wider population.

The main areas of gun regulation concern limiting who can purchase a gun. There have been large majorities in favour of restrictions such as background checks for those with criminal records, limiting access for the mentally ill, and creating a national database to track gun sales. Bans on assault rifles, such as the AR-15, used in Orlando are more controversial. These sorts of weapons were banned in 1994 under the Clinton administration but the law was allowed to lapse in 2004 and stands no chance of being re-enacted by the current Congress.

PARTY LINES

Differing views of gun control across party lines are much more evident now, with Republicans less likely to support a national database or assault weapon ban. These issues have erupted into the presidential campaign. Hillary Clinton called for stronger background checks and a national database, while Donald Trump – who used to support stricter gun control – accepted the endorsement of the National Rifle Association (NRA) and claimed that Clinton "wants to take away Americans' guns". These statements are largely symbolic as neither party appears eager to engage in a strong attempt to enact gun control due to the potential for a backlash from gun enthusiasts.

The most prominent change in state laws regarding guns in recent times has been to make guns more, rather than less, available. In reaction to the massacre at Sandy Hook Elementary School in 2012, Wayne LaPierre, the NTA vice president, argued that "the only thing that will stop a bad guy with a gun is a good guy with a gun".

States adopted this approach, with 41 adopting laws allowing the carrying of concealed guns by 2014. Debates rage over whether this availability makes the public more or less safe, but it is the sharp edge of the current debate in the states. Meanwhile, in Sandy Hook, Newtown – and now Orlando – hundreds of families continue to mourn their dead as mass shootings continue with a dispiriting regularity.

1. How do you interpret the Second Amendment?

"CITING THE CONSTITUTION, GROUPS PREPARE TO DEFEND THEMSELVES AND THEIR RIGHTS," BY ALEX LANCIAL AND JIM TUTTLE, FROM *NEWS21*, AUGUST 16, 2014

Fear of the federal government's interference with Second Amendment rights and suspicion that elected officials are ignoring the "will of the people" have provoked a resurgence of self-described patriots across the country who say they are preparing to defend themselves and their rights by any means necessary.

Organizations tracking the movement say the number of groups has risen dramatically in the past six years.

"There's a very unreasonable, ridiculously crazy attack on the Second Amendment and people that own guns," said Cope Reynolds, a member of the White Mountain Militia in Show Low, Arizona. "If everything were not protected by the Second Amendment, the government would have the opportunity, if they so desired, to go unchecked with impunity and do whatever they want to do."

Reynolds is the operations manager of Shots Ranch, a tactical shooting range and survival training facility in Kingman, Arizona. He considers this type of training to be necessary preparation for a time in America he sees as inevitable.

"We want people to be able to provide for themselves in a world where we might not be able to just run down to Wal-Mart at any time," Reynolds said. "We think that at some point in America we're probably going to experience those times and a lot of us think it's not going to be far away."

For individuals like Reynolds, the Second Amendment is an important check on the government and is needed to protect the Constitution.

"It's the beauty and the danger of America's Constitution," said Adam Winkler, a law professor at the University of California, Los Angeles, and a Second Amendment expert. "Its great generalities are so vague that anyone can interpret them in light of their own experience and their own interests. And indeed, the Second Amendment is one of the most confusing textual provisions of the Constitution."

In 2008, the U.S. Supreme Court ruled in District of Columbia v. Heller that the Second Amendment protects an individual right to own a firearm for traditionally lawful purposes like self-defense.

"It has certainly given fuel to gun rights proponents and to gun culture," said Robert Spitzer, a political scientist, author and professor at State University of New York Cortland who specializes in gun issues. "It fortified, in a very specific way, the very idea that there is in law something called gun rights."

The 2008 ruling held that the individual right to own a firearm is "unconnected with service in a militia."

"There certainly is a belief, and it's a long-standing belief, that somehow average citizens owning guns will somehow have a beneficial or therapeutic effect on government behavior," Spitzer said. "It's rooted in anti-government sentiment, which has a very long history in the U.S."

Reynolds disagrees.

"We're not anti-government. We're anti-corruption in government. There's a huge difference," he said. "We cannot survive without government. We would turn into probably one of the most savage nations on the planet with no government at all."

The Southern Poverty Law Center identified 1,096 "anti-government" patriot groups in the U.S. in its 2013 Intelligence report, an increase from about 150 groups in 2008. Considered part of this movement are 240 militia groups, which the center says have made a resurgence since their earlier popularity in the mid-1990s.

Mark Pitcavage, director of investigative research for the Anti-Defamation League, also has been studying the militia movement for the past 20 years and says the numbers are higher. The ADL keeps an internal list of militia groups, but does not publish it.

"We were tracking around 50 active militia groups in 2008 and now we're tracking between 250 and 300 active militia groups," he said. "It certainly represents a serious surge, which we're able to confirm through the presence of groups and individuals on social networking sites, the number of militia-related events and trainings that we count each year."

Pitcavage said the last militia movement was sparked in part by events in Ruby Ridge, Idaho and Waco, Texas, sieges that tuned in to deadly standoffs with federal agencies. He noted a similarity between these events and the standoff between Cliven Bundy and the Bureau of Land Management earlier this year in Bunkerville, Nevada.

Bundy had been in a disagreement with the government over more than $1 million in grazing fees and fines owed to the federal government. When the BLM came to seize his cattle in April, many militia groups and other members of the patriot movement joined his resistance, aiming their weapons at federal officers until the BLM withdrew.

"Here's someone involved with conflict with the government and the government shows up at his ranch and starts taking his cattle that have been illegally grazing off the property," Pitcavage said. "That's tailor made for the militia movement."

A MODERN MILITIA

Modern private militias are unregulated by the government. Members of the movement say they feel disenfranchised and believe their conservative ideals are at odds with the current administration.

They say that arming themselves and training with other like-minded people gives them a sense of preparedness in an unstable world.

"When I was my kids' age, we never locked the door on our cars, on our houses," said Robert Mitchell, commander of the Citizens Militia of Mississippi. "That doesn't exist anymore. Maybe it sounds cliché, maybe it sounds like Mayberry. I don't know, but that's the way the world's supposed to be. And we have a strong desire to see our communities at least return to that."

A little over a year ago, Mitchell started the Citizens Militia of Mississippi, which now claims nearly 150 official members — a number that members believe would probably be higher if not for the word "militia" in their name. They acknowledged a stigma surrounding the word, and said part of their mission is to help remove the negative connotation.

"Our goal is to change the public opinion of what the militia is," Kevan Owen, commander of the northeast chapter of CMM, said. "We're not a bunch of guys running around the woods, pretending to shoot bad guys."

CMM, which formed in 2013, was not included on the list of anti-government patriot groups published this July by the SPLC. It is one of the newest groups to emerge in the last few years to call itself a militia. Members cite a concern about the current state of our country and a need to defend the Constitution against "enemies foreign and domestic."

"It's supposed to be your neighbors and your friends and your family, working together to better the community," said Doug Jones, the militia's co-founder who also serves as treasurer and second-in-command. "That's really what a militia is."

Active members typically do field training one day a month. That includes drills to practice patrolling and live-fire target practice, as well as learning about first aid, compass navigation and outdoor survival skills. Mitchell says their exercises are largely focused on team building, much like basic training for new military recruits.

Much of their activity focuses on the community. Mitchell said the group holds regular open meetings at the local public library and helps raise money for local police and firefighters.

"We can see ourselves making a difference in our community and in our state. It hasn't been easy," Mitchell said. "It's not going to get easier, but we're going to keep doing it because we can see that result."

While he says he wishes the militia were his full-time job, Mitchell makes his living as a machine operator at Batesville Casket Co. He said most of his remaining time is occupied by CMM business.

"My kids hate it, my ex-wife hates it, my now ex-girl-friend hates it. Everybody in my personal life pretty much hates it, because it consumes all my time," Mitchell said. "It's what I live to do. I'm one of those 'all or nothing' kind of guys, and I've put it all in this."

Mitchell considers the Second Amendment a priority in his life, one that requires sacrifice.

"If you want to get technical about it, every gun law on the books is unconstitutional. I'm not saying give lunatics guns. There have to be limits. Anybody with common sense knows that," Mitchell said. "The problem is, the more you let them infringe on your right, the more they're going to. I'm not willing to let them have any of mine."

Charles Heller is the co-founder of the Arizona Citizens Defense League and spokesman for Jews for the Preservation of Firearms Ownership, a national organiza-tion that aims to "destroy gun control."

The group was formed to spread awareness "about the historical evils that Jews have suffered when they have been disarmed." Twenty-five years later, that mission has expanded.

"I'll put it in four words: Gun control is poison. Any form of gun control," Heller said.

Many gun rights supporters believe that the unin-fringed ability to keep and carry guns is necessary to protect all other rights in the Constitution.

"When the guns are taken away, then the rest of it's all gone," Reynolds said. "There's nothing protecting any of it. The Second Amendment is the glue that holds the Bill of Rights together. If you slide the Second Amendment out of there, the rest of it's going to collapse."

Reynolds is stockpiling food, medical supplies, guns and ammunition for a time when American society collapses. He said such an event happening is "not a matter of if, but when."

People who share these beliefs are preparing throughout the country. A majority of states have at least one established militia group.

In Alaska, militias from across the state have gathered annually for the past three years for a weekend Prepper, Survivalist and Militia Rendezvous just north of Anchorage. The public is invited to come out for "free training provided by patriots." Topics on the training schedule include close-quarter tactics, base defense, camouflage and convoy security.

The Southeast Michigan Volunteer Militia marks its 20th anniversary this year. The group trains every month to prepare for "disasters, crime, invasion, terrorism and tyranny."

This year, its training calendar included topics like winter survival exercises, shotgun and gas mask drills, as well as patrolling in various conditions.

"As 'individual' citizens who have the right to 'keep and bear arms,' we fund our own equipment and arms, we peacefully assemble with other likeminded 'individual' citizens who do the same," said Louis Vondette, a member of SMVM. "We enjoy the best of times, but prepare for the worst of times."

1. The Second Amendment was written to allow militias to self-arm. How do you think this amendment should relate to militia groups today? Are the militia groups that emerge today different from the militias of the eighteenth century?

"SANDY HOOK LAWSUIT IS LATEST EFFORT TO HOLD GUN MAKERS LIABLE FOR MASS SHOOTINGS," BY TIMOTHY D. LYTTON, FROM *THE CONVERSATION* WITH THE SUPPORT OF GEORGIA STATE UNIVERSITY, JUNE 21, 2016

Last year families of the Sandy Hook shooting filed a potentially precedent-setting lawsuit. They sued the manufacturer of the AR-15 rifle that Adam Lanza used to gun down 20 schoolchildren and their teachers in a small town in Connecticut in 2012.

On June 20, lawyers for the gun manufacturers tried to dismiss the suit, arguing that federal law grants them immunity from legal claims arising out of criminal misuse of a weapon.

Although the judge's decision to allow the case to proceed is not expected for several weeks, the litigation highlights the question of whether the gun industry ought to bear some responsibility for helping stem the epidemic of mass shootings that has been sweeping the country. It's a question that has surfaced once more in the immediate aftermath of the tragedy in Orlando.

To many, it seems absurd to hold gun makers liable for marketing a legal product that did precisely what it was designed to do. Although the Second Amendment undoubtedly imposes restrictions on the civil liability of gun manufacturers, the idea of holding them liable for carelessness is actually not so far-fetched.

My research on the history of lawsuits against the gun industry has revealed legal marketing practices that most would agree are irresponsible. For example, some gun manufacturers have sold semiautomatic assault weapons in the form of complete parts kits in order to avoid federally mandated background checks that apply to the sale of firearms but not firearm parts. Others continue to supply retail stores that they know sell hundreds of guns traced to crimes every year.

Holding gun makers liable for such negligent practices would discourage them from circumventing background checks and encourage them to police their supply chain to root out rogue dealers. The problem is they enjoy special immunity under federal law.

The Sandy Hook lawsuit, however, seeks to exploit an exception to this law by putting a novel twist on a traditional legal theory.

OLD AND NEW LEGAL THEORIES

To understand the significance of the Sandy Hook lawsuit, it is helpful to appreciate the history of lawsuits against the gun industry.

Beginning in the 1980s, gun violence victims filed a handful of successful lawsuits against the retail stores that sold the weapons used to injure them under a traditional legal theory called "negligent entrustment."

Under this theory, a person is subject to liability when he entrusts a dangerous object to another who poses a high risk of causing injury with the object. The standard example of negligent entrustment is handing a loaded gun to a small child. In one such case, a woman obtained a US $12 million verdict from Kmart for selling a firearm to a visibly intoxicated person who subsequently shot her.

In the 1990s, gun violence victims began filing lawsuits against firearms manufacturers under a novel theory called "negligent marketing." These lawsuits alleged that careless marketing and distribution practices by gun makers increased the risk their weapons would be criminally misused. For example, the families of victims in a mass shooting alleged that the manufacturer of a semiautomatic weapon designed for close combat-style assaults should have limited the promotion and sale of this weapon to the military and law enforcement.

Courts around the country ultimately rejected these claims. All but a handful were dismissed prior to trial. Of the few cases in which plaintiffs obtained a favorable jury verdict, all were overturned on appeal. Nevertheless, gun violence victims persisted in their efforts to craft a successful legal theory.

In 2005, Congress stepped in to put an end to this litigation by passing the Protection for Lawful Commerce in Arms Act (PLCAA). Under the PLCAA, no court may hold a seller of a gun – whether a retailer or a manufacturer – liable for an injury arising from the criminal misuse of a weapon.

Congress created a number of exceptions to this grant of immunity. One exception, which is especially relevant to the Sandy Hook lawsuit, allows claims based on the theory of negligent entrustment.

Last October, two Milwaukee police officers were awarded $5.6 million in a lawsuit against a gun store using this exception. They proved that the clerk who sold the weapon had facilitated an obvious straw purchase. That is, the clerk sold the gun to an eligible buyer who was acquiring it to give to an ineligible person, who subsequently used it to shoot the officers in the face.

FROM RETAILERS TO MANUFACTURERS

Plaintiffs in the Sandy Hook case are asking the court for the first time to extend the theory of negligent entrustment beyond a retail store to a gun manufacturer.

They argue that the AR-15 is a weapon designed for the military, where soldiers using the gun receive special training and are subject to strict rules regarding appropriate use and safe storage. According to the plaintiffs, facilitating sale of the gun to civilians – who lack the necessary training and rules – is a form of negligent entrustment tantamount to handing the gun to a visibly high-risk individual.

If, as the Sandy Hook plaintiffs argue, marketing the AR-15 to the general public is a form of negligent entrustment, then their claims are not barred by the federal immunity statute.

Lawyers for Bushmaster, which makes the AR-15, have countered that the plaintiffs are merely dressing up a novel negligent marketing claim in traditional negligent entrustment language so as to circumvent Congress' intention to make gun makers immune from civil liability for carelessness in their marketing practices.

BUSINESS AS USUAL?

The case has attracted national media coverage and, in the process, has drawn attention to the role of gun industry marketing and distribution practices in gun violence.

Currently, gun makers do not believe that they bear any responsibility for the lethality of the weapons they sell or for the actions of those who purchase them. A majority of members of Congress appear to agree. It remains to be seen whether the trial judge in the Sandy Hook case holds a different view.

Those who applaud the Sandy Hook lawsuit believe that exposing gun manufacturers to civil liability will encourage them to limit the sale of their most powerful weapons to the military and law enforcement. Critics denounce such efforts as a misuse of the civil justice system – an attempt to promote gun control regulation through private litigation.

The Sandy Hook lawsuit is especially vulnerable to this criticism. Unlike previous attempts to hold gun manufacturers liable for careless marketing practices – such as selling gun kits or supplying weapons to rogue retail dealers – the Sandy Hook plaintiffs' negligent entrustment theory would require a gun maker to refrain altogether from selling a particular weapon. This looks a lot like a gun ban, which is traditionally the province of legislatures.

By contrast, negligent marketing theories that would allow gun makers to sell legal weapons so long as they avoided loopholes in the background check laws and took reasonable measures to police their supply chains would be less likely to run afoul of the separation of powers.

However, Congress precluded these more measured theories of liability when it granted immunity to gun makers. Any revival of these theories would require the repeal of PLCAA.

If the carnage in Sandy Hook, San Bernardino and Orlando has not been enough to move Congress in this direction, it is hard to imagine anything that will.

1. Do you think gun manufacturers should be held legally accountable for mass shootings in which their guns are used? Why or why not?

"OUR GUN-SHY JUSTICES: THE SUPREME COURT ABANDONS THE SECOND AMENDMENT," BY JOSH BLACKMAN, FROM *THE AMERICAN SPECTATOR*, JUNE 23, 2014

After two hundred years of solitude, the Second Amendment now means what it has always said: Our Constitution guarantees the people a right to keep and bear arms. But since *McDonald v. City of Chicago*, the Supreme Court's landmark decision of 2010, the justices seemingly have taken a vow of silence on the meaning of this fundamental right.

Over the last four years, in case after case, lower courts have accepted interpretations of the Second Amendment that have rendered it weak or nonexistent. Each time, a gun control scheme was found constitutional. Each time, once Second Amendment advocates reached the final request for appeal, the Supreme Court declined to review the ruling. With each additional attempt, a sense of déjà vu sets in, always with the same emptiness: "The petition for a writ of certiorari is denied." There is no indication whether the lower courts are right or wrong, whether they have strayed from precedent or followed it faithfully. The Supreme Court, content with the status quo, has knowingly and willingly abandoned the Second Amendment to the judges below.

In the 2008 Case *District of Columbia v. Heller*, the Supreme Court invalidated D.C.'s complete ban on the ownership of handguns. For the first time in its existence, the Court recognized a constitutional guarantee to individual ownership of a firearm. But the legal battle was just getting started.

Because *Heller* nixed only a federal law covering D.C., a second ruling was needed to determine whether the right would extend (or be "incorporated," in legal lingo) to the states. Thus, immediately after *Heller* was decided, a follow-up lawsuit was filed in Chicago, challenging the Windy City's hand-gun ban. In 2010, the Supreme Court ruled in *McDonald v. City of Chicago* that the right to keep and bear arms protected by *Heller* did indeed apply to the states as well. Chicago's ban on handguns went out the window.

Second Amendment advocates, now two for two before the high court, drew up a comprehensive, multi-stage litigation strategy to challenge various types of gun regulations: licensing regimes that bar or unreasonably burden

carrying firearms outside the home; excessively high registration fees; onerous registration requirements; restrictions
unduly infringing the sale of firearms; and countless others.
It was understood that this litigation would take time, and
that different courts of appeals would likely split and fracture
on the questions in various ways. But the plan all along was
that the Supreme Court would take one case at a time and
incrementally clarify the scope of gun rights—starting with
the threshold issue of whether the Second Amendment even
applies outside the home. Indeed, this is the Court's preferred
path in many other contexts: Hand down a broad ruling, wait
for arguments over the minutiae to trickle back up, and then
clarify. Patience is the name of the game.

But this patience has been met with total silence.
In the four years since *McDonald*, citizens denied
the right to bear arms outside the home have challenged gun control laws in California, Illinois, Maryland,
Massachusetts, New Jersey, New York, and elsewhere.
Lower courts have grappled with the meaning and scope
of *Heller*, and implored the high court for further guidance,
but to no avail. The Second Amendment is trapped somewhere between legal limbo and constitutional purgatory.

Let's examine eight of the most high-profile cases
that the justices turned away:

1. In *Williams v. Maryland* (2010), the Maryland
Court of Appeals limited the Second Amendment to the
four walls of one's home, finding that the right to bear
arms elsewhere was "outside the scope of the Second
Amendment." Pleading for clarification from the justices, the
court concluded, "If the Supreme Court ... meant its holding
[in *Heller* and *McDonald*] to extend beyond home possession,

it will need to say so more plainly." The Court did not speak plainly, since it denied review on October 3, 2011.

2. In *United States v. Masciandaro* (2010), the Fourth Circuit Court of Appeals similarly declined to recognize a Second Amendment right to bear arms outside the home: "On the question of *Heller*'s applicability outside the home environment, we think it prudent to await direction from the Court itself" Imprudently offering no direction, the Supreme Court denied review on November 28, 2011.

3. The Second Circuit Court of Appeals, in *Kachalsky v. Westchester County* (2012), upheld New York's onerous handgun licensing system, which requires an "applicant to demonstrate 'proper cause' to obtain a license to carry a concealed handgun in public." This "proper cause" mandates that a person jump through countless hoops to exercise his constitutional right of self defense. The Second Circuit, like its sister courts, recognized that *Heller* "raises more questions than it answers." The Supreme Court let them remain unanswered and denied review on April 15, 2013.

4. In *Woodard v. Gallagher* (2012), the Fourth Circuit Court of Appeals upheld Maryland's handgun licensing rules that limit the right to carry a concealed weapon to those who have proven a "good and substantial reason." Letting that assumption stand, or maybe not, the Supreme Court denied review on October 15, 2013.

5. In *Chardin v. Police Commissioner of Boston* (2013), in the absence of clear standards, the judges

"merely assume[d] that the *Heller* right exists outside the home." the Massachusetts Supreme Judicial Court upheld the Common-Wealth's firearm licensing statute, which requires an applicant to show a "good reason to fear injury to his person or property." The ruling found that this high burden "does not infringe on a right protected by the Second Amendment." Without comment, the Supreme Court denied review on November 4, 2013.

6 & 7. In *National Rifle Association v. McCraw* (2013), the Fifth Circuit Court of Appeals upheld a Texas law denying the right to carry handguns outside the home to those between the ages of eighteen and twenty. The court based its ruling on a previous decision, *NRA v. Bureau of Alcohol Tobacco, Firearms, and Explosives* (2012), finding constitutional a federal law that bans adults between those ages from purchasing handguns. Six judges from the court who dissented on the latter case wanted it to be reheard and found the implications of the majority's reading of *Heller* "far-reaching" and "simply wrong." They lost by a margin of one vote. Right or wrong, we cannot know—the Supreme Court simply denied review of both cases on February 24, 2014.

8. *Drake v. Jerejian* (2013) is the most recent appellate decision that upheld a draconian limitation on the right to bear arms. New Jersey is a "may issue" state, meaning that a license to carry a firearm outside the home *may* only be granted if the applicant proves a "justifiable need," as determined by law enforcement. This is a high burden, which requires the applicant to show a specific, immediate threat to his safety, and to demonstrate that the *only* way to avoid

that threat is by carrying a firearm, as opposed to calling 911. Even assuming the police chief grants the permit—which seldom happens—the process is not over. Next, the applicant must appear before a judge to state his case. To make it even tougher, the local prosecutor can oppose the permit. And even if the applicant can navigate this labyrinth, the permit is only valid for two years, and the process must be begun over from scratch. If the right to keep and bear arms means anything outside the home, this gauntlet could not possibly be constitutional. Yet, remarkably, the Third Circuit Court of Appeals upheld this tortuous process. The impossible-to-satisfy burden of seeking the approval of two branches of New Jersey's government, the court found, "does not burden conduct within the scope of the Second Amendment." Effectively, carrying a firearm outside the home is beyond the "scope" of the Second Amendment. Over a strong dissent, the majority "decline[d] to definitively declare that the individual right to bear arms for the purpose of self-defense extends beyond the home." Continuing its practice, on May 5, 2014, the Supreme Court denied review.

There are hundreds of other ongoing challenges to gun laws, and lower courts across the country are continuing to weigh in on the Second Amendment without guidance from the Supreme Court. And, in virtually every single case, the lower courts have upheld restrictions on the right to keep and bear arms. According to the Brady Center to Prevent Gun Violence, since *Heller* there have been 800 challenges to gun laws, and the lower courts have upheld 96 percent of them. The Supreme Court, with the exception of *McDonald*, has not deemed a single case worthy of reconsideration.

Several of the cases mentioned earlier involved messy facts—defendants, for example, who had been convicted of gun crimes. This may have given the justices reason enough to pass. The principles may have been worthy of debate, but the cases suffered what are known in business as "vehicle problems." But many of the recent petitions were well-crafted "test cases." They were designed by organizations—the National Rifle Association, the Second Amendment Foundation--that know how to present issues to the justices cleanly. The cases were brought against the most onerous gun regulations, with law-abiding plaintiffs, in jurisdictions where the legal issue had not yet been settled. Yet the Court has continued to demur.

Alan Gura, the attorney who successfully argued *Heller* and *McDonald* before the Supreme Court, places the impact of these unguided lower court opinions in context. "Unless the Supreme Court decides to enforce its pronouncements, the Second Amendment will apply only to the extent that some lower courts are willing to honor Supreme Court precedent." In other words, the Second Amendment means different things to different people in different states, at the discretion of lower court judges. This is not how any other fundamental constitutional rights work.

But gun control advocates have taken this as encouragement. Jonathan Lowy of the Brady Center has said that that the Court's refusal to take any Second Amendment cases reaffirms its "satisfaction with lower courts upholding all gun laws that have been challenged, so long as they allow responsible citizens to keep a gun in the home." The Brady Center's research arm notes that, "These denials make clear that states still retain the discretion to pass strong laws regulating the carrying of firearms in public even after the *Heller* decision."

Generally, when the Court denies review of a given case, it is a fool's errand to try to figure out why. But when the Court denies, in sequence, many cases that address the same constitutional issue, one that has divided lower courts, a pattern becomes clear. So what do we make of the Supreme Court standing idly by while other judges fire away at the right to keep and bear arms?

It only takes four justices to grant *certiorari* on a case, in contrast with the five votes needed to craft a majority opinion. Perhaps there are four justices who would rule that the Second Amendment protects a right to carry outside the home, but those same justices know that there are also five votes to place a limit on the Second Amendment. Perhaps, then, four or five justices would rather maintain the awkward status quo than see *Heller* rolled back.

All hope is not lost, though. There are several cases still in the Second Amendment pipeline (or barrel, as it were) that will afford the Supreme Court an opportunity to rectify the situation. In *Peruta v. County of San Diego*, a divided panel of the Ninth Circuit Court of Appeals found that the Second Amendment protects the right to a handgun carry license. The court threw out San Diego's system that required applicants to demonstrate "good cause" prior to receiving permits.

In an odd procedural move, California Attorney General Kamala Harris (who was not a party in the proceedings) intervened, and asked the entire Ninth Circuit to rehear the case. If this petition is granted, a nine-judge panel of the Ninth Circuit, known as an *en banc* court, will rehear the case. The decision may well be reversed, and the *en banc* Ninth Circuit may in turn uphold the law. If this comes to pass, as I suspect it will, then at some point in 2015 *Peruta* will land, like so many cases before it, at the steps of 1 First Street NE, Washington, D.C.

But if the Supreme Court denies review in *Peruta*, we may find ourselves running out of options. By ignoring this issue, the Court will have left the Second Amendment to wither on the vine. The right to keep and bear arms will be reduced to a hollow privilege in many states. Regardless of how the Court would resolve the tangled mess of lower precedents, the failure to even confront it, and rule on it, stands as a jurisprudential abdication of the Second Amendment.

1. Do you share the author's suspicion that the Supreme Court's holding pattern is because the four pro-gun justices fear the Heller decision will be overturned? How do you see this playing out?

2. Many of the legal challenges surround carrying a weapon outside the home. Do you feel the Second Amendment extends this right to law-abiding citizens? Or do you think gun owners should be required to demonstrate a clear threat to carry a gun in public?

CHAPTER 4

WHAT ADVOCACY GROUPS SAY

Progressive measures to reduce gun violence—and the inevitable conservative pushback against them—typically play out on the advocacy front, at least initially. The various interest groups seeking new gun laws, and those who wish to prevent any such action, have an immense interest in steering public opinion in one direction or the other with respect to guns.

The National Rifle Association (NRA) has historically dominated public discourse on gun rights. With an operating budget of around a quarter of a billion dollars, the group's PR campaigns have proven extremely effective (or obstructionist, depending on one's view) in defeating any congressional legislation. Following their lead, other vocal groups such as Gun Owners of America push for a "no-compromise" interpretation of the Second Amendment. While their rhetoric lacks subtlety, there is little doubt their tactics, and lobbying dollars, work.

There is evidence however that the public mood on guns is changing, and new interest groups advocating for stricter gun laws are capitalizing on this shift. Everytown for Gun Safety is a powerful gun control advocacy group formed in 2014, and backed by former NYC mayor and billionaire Michael Bloomberg. This group recommended executive action to circumvent a Republican congress adverse to any new gun laws. In January 2016, Obama proposed sweeping action on guns. Whether these will survive inevitable legal challenges remain to be seen.

"DEBATE HAS CHANGED SINCE NEWTOWN, BUT NOT ALWAYS IN PREDICTABLE WAYS," BY JUSTINE MCDANIEL, ALLISON GRINER, AND NATALIE KREBS, *NEWS21*, AUGUST 16, 2014

Twenty months after the mass shooting at Sandy Hook Elementary School in Newtown, Connecticut, some would say little has changed when it comes to guns in America.

Others would say everything has.

Flurries of gun-related legislation and renewed national attention on the topic have not been enough to change federal gun laws. The National Rifle Association, still the most powerful entity in the war over guns in America, no longer has a monopoly on the debate.

A resurgence of the gun control movement is challenging the status quo, while groups to the right of the NRA are also growing. Nonprofit organizations on each side are battling like they haven't in years, all trying to shape the country's politics and win over the American people.

But in spite of the evolving landscape, no progress in either direction is certain.

The gun control movement was nearly $285 million behind the gun rights movement in 2012 revenue raised, before Sandy Hook. Today, it is playing catch-up to the money, membership and political savvy of its opponents as the NRA works to maintain its dominance.

Over the course of this year, News21 reporters, videographers and photojournalists traveled across the country to assess the state of the gun debate, its evolution and emerging issues.

With new groups, a revamped strategy, more money and unprecedented collaboration, the gun control movement has made headway. Organizations like Everytown for Gun Safety, the group backed by former New York City Mayor Michael Bloomberg, say they are moving the needle.

"Now, for the first time in our country's history, there is a well-financed and formidable force positioned to take on the Washington gun lobby," said Shannon Watts, founder of gun control group Moms Demand Action for Gun Sense in America, speaking at an Everytown event on Capitol Hill in May.

Whether that is possible remains to be seen.

The NRA is strong financially. Its budget has consistently hovered well above $200 million in revenue in recent years and it has cultivated a highly organized grassroots base for more than a century.

As the gun control movement organized in the wake of Sandy Hook, the gun rights movement's membership boomed. Groups more conservative than the NRA, like the National Association for Gun Rights, are growing. State legislatures across the country passed laws expanding gun rights. The NRA has focused on broadening its appeal.

The NRA frequently targets Bloomberg, who donated $50 million to Everytown in April, though the amount is a quarter of what the NRA raises each year.

"Mr. Bloomberg, you're an arrogant hypocrite," said NRA Institute for Legislative Action Executive Director Chris Cox at the organization's annual convention in April. "Stay out of our homes, stay out of our refrigerators and stay the hell out of our gun cabinets."

With its near-mythical presence as a political lobby, the NRA is still the best-positioned player in the debate by far, bringing in and spending hundreds of millions of dollars on its broad range of programs. Though its grip on Congress has loosened somewhat, it still isn't letting major federal legislation through or relinquishing its influence on state politics.

An amendment expanding background checks came to a vote in the Senate in April 2013, something gun control advocates saw as a victory. It didn't get enough votes to pass.

The NRA began as a firearms education organization and sportsmen's club in 1871 and didn't become involved in politics until the 1970s. When it did, however, it had a built-in base of support. It has worked to build strong ties with members of Congress to back its lobbying and political efforts. Today, the NRA says it has 5 million members.

Around the same time the NRA entered politics, the group that would eventually become the Brady Campaign to Prevent Gun Violence was founded. It attained a high profile following the 1981 assassination attempt on President Ronald Reagan, in which Reagan press secretary James Brady was shot and partially paralyzed. Brady died this summer; his death has been ruled a homicide.

Its advocacy work in the '80s and '90s culminated in the passage of the Brady Act — which mandated federal background checks on people buying firearms — and the now-expired assault-weapons ban, both signed by President Bill Clinton in 1994.

In 1999, the Columbine High School shooting led to a resurgence of gun control advocacy. Like today's movement, it had a billionaire benefactor in Monster.com's Andrew J. McKelvey and a mother-led group, the Million Mom March. After a handful of state legislative victories, the movement fizzled.

This was the landscape when a spate of recent prominent mass shootings began: Virginia Tech in 2007; Tucson, Arizona, in 2011, in which former Congresswoman Gabrielle Giffords, an Arizona Democrat, was shot; the Aurora, Colorado, movie theater shooting in 2012; and then, Newtown.

The Sandy Hook shooting touched off for the gun control side what Everytown Director of Strategy and Partnerships Brina Milikowsky called a "once-in-a-generation moment of great transformation."

The day after the shooting, Watts founded Moms Demand Action; a few weeks later, on the second anniversary of the Tucson shooting, Giffords and her husband, Mark Kelly, started Americans for Responsible Solutions.

In December 2013, Moms Demand Action formed a partnership with Mayors Against Illegal Guns, a group founded in 2006 by Bloomberg and former Boston Mayor Thomas Menino. In April, Everytown became an umbrella organization for the two other groups. Today, Everytown says it has 2 million members.

"Twenty years ago, Brady was the only game in town. And now there's unprecedented resources and attention being focused on this issue, so we're not a voice alone in the wilderness anymore," said Dan Gross, president of the Brady Campaign.

In fact, there is a profusion of gun control groups, including many on the state level.

November's congressional elections — the first major election since Sandy Hook — could provide a barometer for the political gun wars.

Some groups, like Moms Demand Action and the Brady Campaign, say they can now compete with the gun lobby. Others, like Giffords' ARS, say they want to match the NRA but are still too new to have a comparable budget.

With new strategies, groups like the Coalition to Stop Gun Violence, founded in 1974, think they will "be a force for decades to come," said Ladd Everitt, the group's director of communications.

But tax filings show the top six national gun rights groups brought in close to $301 million in revenue in 2012, while six major national gun control nonprofits raised just more than $16 million.

The dollars are hard to track. The most recent tax filings available are from 2012, so they don't reflect any changes that have occurred since Newtown, including Bloomberg's $50 million donation to Everytown.

Nonprofits are not required to disclose information about their donors.

Because Everytown, Moms Demand Action and Americans for Responsible Solutions are so new, their tax forms are not available yet.

However, when it comes to campaign spending, the political action committees on the two sides are neck-and-neck for 2014.

As of June 30, the NRA PAC had just more than $18 million in receipts and the ARS PAC had almost $17.5 million. ARS had spent nearly $8.5 million; the NRA had spent nearly $2.7 million, according to filings with the Federal Election Commission.

With some groups' finances remaining a mystery, the numbers are inconclusive. In spite of their claims, gun control groups' ability to compete financially remains questionable.

"We don't have as much evidence as people some-times think we do that you can sort of throw money at your cause and get your way," said Matt Grossmann, a political science professor at Michigan State University. "In fact, that hardly ever works, especially for advocacy groups."

Much of the NRA's power is found in its passionate and faithful membership base.

"Their members are very highly trained in grassroots campaigning, so because of the emotional connection to guns, they are easily activated, and that is certainly a plus on their side," said Karen Callaghan, a political science professor at Texas Southern University who is writing a book on the NRA.

Their members are loyal and, often, lifelong. For many, the organization offers a mark of identity.

"When the person's a member of the NRA, most people know what that is. It speaks volumes of how they stand on issues, and it's respected or hated by almost everybody," said Brad Leeser, 58, a member of the NRA and Gun Owners of America in Moorhead, Minnesota.

Gun rights voters tend to be single-issue voters, meaning they prioritize gun rights over all other issues. Gun control supporters, on the other hand, tend to be less driven by the one issue.

"People on the other side of the debate, it's a more diffused group, and so I think they're disempowered for that reason," said Kathy Kiely, managing editor of the Sunlight Foundation, a nonpartisan open-government nonprofit.

In July, the NRA started its 2014 "Trigger the Vote" campaign, an effort to get pro-gun voters to register before the November election. When Everytown was founded, it launched a "gun-sense voter" campaign, which aims to get "voters to consider gun-violence prevention as a number-one issue that they vote on," said Jennifer Hoppe, program director for Moms Demand Action.

"The NRA and the gun lobby have done an amazing job over the last 30 years … changing hearts and minds at every level up to the Supreme Court," said Shaun Dakin, a volunteer who works with organizations including Moms Demand Action and the Brady Campaign. "Now the gun-violence-prevention movement has figured that out … Washington, D.C., will change when the culture changes and when they see people actually voting based on any particular issue."

Building a grassroots effort is part of the gun control movement's attempt to attract supporters and compete with the NRA.

That was Watts' goal in founding Moms Demand Action, which the Indiana mother of five modeled after Mothers Against Drunk Driving. It became a leading grassroots gun control organization and now has chapters in all 50 states.

"For the first time ever, there is a grassroots group that is going toe-to-toe with the gun lobby. That's never been the case before," Watts said in an interview in May.

Moms Demand Action's strategy includes calling legislators, holding rallies — like a June march across the Brooklyn Bridge — and putting pressure on corporations and politicians through social media.

This type of organization is seen in the movement as a whole. The groups have begun to collaborate to move closer to a united front similar to that of the NRA membership base.

Each group plays a specific role, though almost all of them focus on political advocacy at the federal and state levels. The major national groups have a weekly conference call to discuss priorities and plans. Combined, the groups' strategy covers legislation tracking, legal work, data collection and research, gun-safety education, work with survivors and more.

"There's never been a point in history ... where this movement's been more unified," Everitt, of the Coalition to Stop Gun Violence, said. "There's a lot of mutual respect in our movement and even love."

The newcomer groups are joined by more established organizations like the Law Center to Prevent Gun Violence, the Coalition to Stop Gun Violence, the National

Gun Victims Action Council, the Brady Campaign and Brady Center.

There is no clear leader in the movement. Once the most powerful, the Brady Campaign sees itself as a gathering point for others now, but collaboration, not star power, is the key, Gross, president of the Brady Campaign, said.

Everytown, the newest player, has perhaps the biggest presence in the news and is the largest of the advocacy groups. Milikowsky says the group leads in research, investigation and thought, but it doesn't view itself as the leader.

"The only way we're going to overcome the corporate gun lobby, the only way we're going to change deeply entrenched social norms, is not to be about any one organization but be about the American public," Gross said.

Among the gun rights groups, the NRA overshadows other organizations, but many groups want better collaboration.

"We work together when possible, but we don't always communicate as well as we probably should," said Alan Gottlieb, chairman of the Citizens Committee for the Right to Keep and Bear Arms and the founder of the Second Amendment Foundation.

Luke Wagner, a grassroots activist who is now the board president of the Colorado Second Amendment Association, said he works to develop ties with other gun rights groups.

"We don't have to be intrinsically tied to one another. We don't have to take instructions from one another. But we do have to be able to talk to one another and at least be sure we're all on the same page," Wagner said.

Though some groups want more collaboration, gun rights organizations positioning themselves as alternatives to the NRA have grown financially in recent years.

Groups like Gun Owners of America, which opposes all gun control measures unequivocally, and the National Association for Gun Rights, a newcomer that is blatantly anti-NRA, are trying to challenge the older organization.

NAGR's revenue grew 16 times from 2009 to 2012, an increase unparalleled by fellow gun rights organizations. Gun Owners of America's revenue grew from about $1.8 million in 2011 to $2.4 million in 2012.

"The NRA has taken gun owners' money and more importantly, their trust and used it to support those who have a horrible record when it comes to gun rights," according to one NAGR press release. The group did not respond to requests for comment for this story.

In May, the NRA called the tactics of another gun rights group, Open Carry Texas, "downright weird." After protest from the group, which carries long guns in public to protest the Texas ban on the open carry of handguns, the NRA pulled the release from its website and replaced it with a message of unity.

The NRA did not respond to requests for comment.

For advocates like Nicki Kenyon, a writer for Jews for the Preservation of Firearm Ownership and a former editor of an NRA magazine, the gun rights movement's theme is unity of mission, if not unity in tactics.

"We may go about it in different ways. We may disagree on the tactics. But overall, we are an inclusive and we are a cohesive group of people whose only purpose is to protect our rights and freedoms," she said.

But these groups are still small players compared to the NRA.

"The NRA is seen as the voice of gun owners. It doesn't necessarily need much help," said Grossmann, the Michigan State University professor.

Modern gun rights advocacy experienced a turning point after the Supreme Court ruled in District of Columbia v. Heller in 2008 that the right to bear arms is an individual right, not limited to those serving in a militia.

The decision overturned handgun bans on state and local levels, and groups like the Second Amendment Foundation followed it with their own lawsuits to reverse gun control measures in major cities like Chicago.

It brought a new sense of security to gun rights advocates.

"It's having a huge impact, and the other side will … deny it or try to spin it a certain way, but they know they're losing," said Philip Watson, director of special projects for the Second Amendment Foundation.

After Heller, the NRA began opening up to new demographics, said Callaghan, the Texas Southern University political science professor.

In the last few years, it has launched social media campaigns aimed at millennials, women and minorities. It recently debuted a show on its website hosted by a young black gun enthusiast and has six social media accounts aimed just at women.

Both sides of the debate want to reframe the conversation to use less loaded language and portray their stances as common sense.

Americans for Responsible Solutions is one of the groups trying to depoliticize the debate. Giffords and her husband, both gun owners, hoped to establish a presence that would counterbalance the NRA while welcoming gun owners, said Mark Prentice, the group's press secretary.

"It's about staking a place in the kind of moderate, reasonable middle where most people are on this issue," Prentice said.

But what is described as common sense for one side is not common sense for the other.

For example, many gun rights advocates portray "stand your ground" laws, which allow people to use deadly force in self-defense instead of retreating, as common sense; gun control groups oppose it. Gun control groups say expanding background checks is common sense; gun rights groups disagree.

Mental health may be the one area that has the potential to be a meeting ground.

The NRA has supported mental health legislation in the past, like the 2007 law meant to improve state reporting to the National Instant Criminal Background Check System (NICS), which includes the reporting of mental health records. The Brady Campaign also worked to pass that bill.

In May, a combination mental health and domestic violence bill was introduced in the House by Democratic Reps. Mike Thompson of California and Elizabeth Esty of Connecticut, whose district includes Newtown. It is still in committee.

In the same month, an amendment to increase funding for NICS by $19.5 million in 2015 passed the House, but the Senate has not taken it up. The amendment's passage was seen as a victory by the gun control movement — its single federal legislative success since Newtown — but NICS funding will not actually increase unless the bill passes the Senate.

The gun control movement also wants legislation addressing domestic abuse and background checks. Advocates still hope for expanded background checks that would include sales online and at gun shows. A bill like that failed in Congress last year.

Congresswoman Carolyn McCarthy, a Democrat from New York, whose husband was killed in a commuter train shooting in 1993, has been a vocal gun control advocate in Congress since the 1990s.

"So many members in the House and the Senate started to stand up and speak, so there's so many more voices out there today than there was even 10 years ago," McCarthy said at a February Moms Demand Action news conference on Capitol Hill.

"We went through at least a decade, if not more, where we were not political enough, where PACs we once had that were raising money ... folded. We didn't have a financial presence in elections," said Everitt of the Coalition to Stop Gun Violence. "We weren't playing hardball."

But given gridlock in Congress, both sides are fighting battles on other fronts, particularly in the states.

"We've shifted some of our priorities, and while we're still leading the fight in Congress to strengthen our federal gun laws, we are doing more and more advocacy work at the state level and working to strengthen state gun laws," said Everytown's Milikowsky.

Six states passed laws this year to help remove firearms from domestic abusers. In Minnesota Everytown helped draft the bill.

Since the Heller ruling, the NRA has helped pass laws regarding concealed carry of guns, self-defense and "stand your ground," often fighting multiple battles on the state level, said Callaghan, the political science professor. Grassroots gun rights groups often help or launch their own legislative campaigns.

Last year in Colorado, voters recalled some legislators who passed a package of gun control laws. The campaign was led by a citizen movement called the Basic Freedom Defense Fund.

The NRA eventually joined the campaign, but it was spearheaded by the grassroots activists, something that often happens at the state level.

As the political tug-of-war continues, an indicator of the future of guns in America is elusive. Many are looking to the 2014 elections for a hint.

The NRA's Cox said on an NRA commentary show that the upcoming election is crucial.

"There's no question that what we do between now and November is critical to the survival of the Second Amendment and the freedoms we all fight so hard to protect," Cox said.

The NRA rates candidates and endorses them through its PAC. According to the fund, the rankings are based on voting records, public statements and responses to a questionnaire, the contents of which the NRA does not release publicly.

The association worked on 271 campaigns for Congress in 2008 and says it won 230 of the races, according to its website. Voters can print out "personal voting cards" from the website that list the candidates and mark which are supported by the NRA.

In July, Everytown sent out a questionnaire to every candidate for Congress. It is similar to the NRA's, but unlike the NRA, Everytown released the questions to make its process transparent. Milikowsky and other representatives would not say whether the group will make election endorsements, nor would they say what it will do with the survey results beyond publishing them.

Prentice, of Americans for Responsible Solutions, believes the issue of guns is going to be increasingly important in elections, and said his organization sees it as an obligation to highlight the issue and the candidates' stances in campaigns around the country. The group doesn't donate directly to candidates, but plans to channel money into ads supporting certain candidates.

"What's most important is the people who have been champions on this issue already and (who) put their necks out there get to return to the U.S. Congress," Prentice said.

"The election is going to be a bare-knuckles street fight," said NRA Executive Vice President and CEO Wayne LaPierre at the organization's convention. "They're going after every House seat, every Senate seat, every governor's chair, every statehouse that they can get their hands on."

Jacob Byk contributed to this story.

1. How can gun law advocacy groups compete with big-budget gun rights groups like the NRA? Does this boil down to a story of who has the most money to spend on their campaign?

"DEBATE: IS STRICT GUN CONTROL THE BEST WAY TO PREVENT SHOOTINGS? ANOTHER MASSACRE BEGS WHAT CAN BE DONE," FROM *PANAM POST*, JUNE 30, 2015

"BRADY BACKGROUND CHECKS SAVE LIVES," BY JONATHAN HUTSON

Every day in the United States, 89 people are killed with guns. Most of these tragedies can be prevented by keeping guns out of the wrong hands through common-sense solutions supported by the vast majority of US Americans.

Right now, in most of our nation, a convicted felon, a domestic abuser, a fugitive, or someone who has been judged dangerously mentally ill can walk into a gun show, or go online, and buy a gun with no questions asked — without a Brady background check. This is unacceptable.

Since the Brady Law was passed with bipartisan support in 1994, 2.4 million dangerous people have been blocked from buying guns. So a simple solution is for the US Congress to expand Brady background checks to all gun sales in order to prevent millions of guns from winding up in dangerous hands.

This is an issue of public health and safety, on which the vast majority of US Americans agree. Ninety percent of the public, including 85 percent of gun owners, support the expansion of life-saving Brady background checks to all gun sales.

So people from all states and political parties are signing our #IamCharleston: "I Demand a Vote NOW" petition, demanding that Congress "finish the job" by voting immediately in support of legislation to expand Brady background checks to all gun sales.

Every day that Congress fails to act, more guns get into dangerous hands, and every day, more lives are lost as a result. We also need to do more to stop "bad-apple" gun dealers — the 5 percent of dealers who knowingly or negligently supply 90 percent of the crime guns in our nation.

Through organizing protests in front of "bad-apple" gun-dealer stores, and through legal advocacy, Brady is pressuring the "bad apples" to either adopt a reasonable and ethical Code of Conduct, or be shut down.

But policy solutions are not our only focus. We know that every day in the United States, nine kids are shot unintentionally. So through our ASK (Asking Saves Kids) Campaign, we're educating parents about the risks of unsafe access to guns in the home, and how to mitigate those risks. In two-thirds of school shootings, the gun comes from the home of the attacker or a relative, including the December 2012 shooting at Sandy Hook in Newtown, Connecticut.

One in three homes with children in the US have guns, many unlocked and loaded. So one simple, life-saving question that every parent should ask before their kids have a playdate is whether there are unlocked guns where their kids play.

Through simple, common-sense solutions, supported by nearly all US Americans, including the vast majority of gun owners, the Brady Campaign plans to realize the audacious but achievable goal of cutting gun deaths in half in the United States by 2025.

Jonathan Hutson, J.D. is a communications strategist and former investigative journalist. He works as chief communications officer for the Brady Campaign and Center to Prevent Gun Violence in Washington, DC. Follow @jonhutson.

"GUN CONTROL HELPS SHOOTERS, NOT VICTIMS," BY JOHN LOTT

With just two exceptions, since at least 1950, all the mass public shootings in the United States have occurred in so-called gun-free zones, places where citizens can't have guns for protection. Gun-free zones are rare in the United States, but those are the places where these killers go time after time.

There is a reason why every city or country around the world that has banned guns has seen its murder rates rise. Law-abiding citizens, not criminals, obey these bans. Instead of making places safer, disarming law abiding citizens left them sitting ducks.

The vast majority of mass public shooters in the United States kill people to get attention. They want to commit suicide, but they want to do so in a way that will get them attention, so people will know that they have been here. The more people that they can kill, the more attention they will receive.

Mass public killers constantly talk about finding places where their victims are easy targets. This month's killer of nine people at a Charleston church initially considered targeting the College of Charleston, but decided against it because it had security personnel.

Last June, Elliot Rodger, who killed six people in Santa Barbara, California, explained his own choice. In his 141-page "manifesto," Rodger turned down targets because he worried that someone with a gun would stop his killing spree.

That same month, Justin Bourque in Canada shot three people to death. His Facebook page made fun of gun bans, with pictures of defenseless victims explaining to killers that they weren't allowed to have guns.

The diary of the Aurora, Colorado, Batman movie-theater killer, James Holmes, was just released a month ago. He was considering both attacking an airport and a movie theater, but he turned down the airport option because of their "substantial security." Out of the seven theaters showing the Batman movie premiere within 20 minutes of Holmes's apartment, only one banned permitted concealed handguns. He didn't go to the closest nor the largest, but to the one that banned self-defense.

Wanting easy targets is understandable. There is a long list of mass public shootings that have been stopped by citizens with permitted concealed handguns; though when people stop these attacks, they don't get much media attention.

With mass public shooters planning these attacks for at least six months in advance, attackers have plenty of time to figure out how to obtain a gun. Background checks rarely work. The terrorists who attacked France in January were armed with numerous semi-automatic handguns, automatic Kalashnikov rifles, an M42 rocket launcher, 10 Molotov cocktails, 10 smoke grenades, a hand grenade, and 15 sticks of dynamite. So much for the country's ban on all these items.

Despite strict gun control, seven European countries have a higher death rate from mass public shootings than the United States.

Ask yourself: would you feel safer with a sign on your home saying "this house is a gun-free zone"? But if you wouldn't put these signs on your home, why put them elsewhere?

John Lott is the president of the Crime Prevention Research Center, and the author of **More Guns, Less Crime.** *Follow @JohnRLottJr.*

1. Which argument seems most convincing to you? Why?

"PUBLIC HEALTH TAKING STRONGER APPROACH TO GUN VIOLENCE: APHA, BRADY TEAM UP ON PREVENTION," BY LINDSEY WAHOWIAK, FROM *THE NATION'S HEALTH*, JANUARY 2016

Public health advocates can agree that shootings are a huge health issue, considering the more than 33,000 deaths from gun violence in 2014 alone. But gun violence also indicates community-wide health issues, according to researchers.

To a packed crowd at a session at APHA's 143rd Annual Meeting and Exposition, advocates from the Brady Campaign to Prevent Gun Violence and other public health fields gathered to discuss how to create a public health movement to address gun violence. The tools are already in place, but much work still needs to be done, as 11 children are killed with a gun every day in the U.S., said David Hemenway, professor of Health Policy and Director of the Harvard Injury Control Research Center and APHA member.

Violence begets violence, noted epidemiologist and APHA member Gary Slutkin, MD, but communities can do their parts to mitigate violence. It will take looking at gun violence in new ways — as a public health issue, rather than a criminal justice issue, he said.

"Criminal justice reform won't be enough," Slutkin said. "(We need to) go harder at prevention, harder at understanding, harder at care."

The session touched on many points the Brady Campaign has been touting for years, including at its

National Summit with APHA in October in Washington, D.C. The partnership between APHA and the Brady Campaign was facilitated in large part by APHA's Maternal and Child Health Section's Gun Violence Prevention Committee, and grew from a joint forum held in March last year. Dan Gross, the campaign's president, led the charge on the organization's three key points, calling for policymakers to:

- finish the job of expanding "lifesaving Brady background checks" to all gun sales in the U.S.,
- stop "bad apple" gun dealers and
- "ASK," part of Asking Saves Kids, or asking families if guns are in their homes before allowing kids to play there.

"This is a new day for the gun violence issue," Gross told attendees at the summit. "The tipping point for our issue has finally arrived. The American public, everyone, is finally coming together to say, 'enough.'"

Georges Benjamin, MD, executive director of APHA, said it is time to address gun violence from a prevention approach, rather than responding to violence after the fact. During the summit, Benjamin called on all sectors to join the public health community in partnering for stronger prevention models and practice. "I think we need a private, privately funded research initiative to help us answer a lot of these questions as we go forward so we can be more data-driven," he said. "Public health can bring these things to the table."

Obstacles, however, remain. On Dec. 3 — the day after a mass shooting in San Bernardino, California, took the life of 14 health department workers — the U.S. Senate voted down a bipartisan amendment that would have expanded gun sale background checks to gun shows and online sales.

Attitudes influenced by the gun lobby are also a roadblock to stemming the rate of gun violence. According to Brady Campaign data, in 2004, 42 percent of Americans believed a gun made a home safer. By 2014, that number jumped to 63 percent, despite scientific evidence to the contrary. A study published in 2004 in the *American Journal of Epidemiology* found that families that had purchased a handgun were linked to an elevated risk of both homicide and suicide.

Suicide, in fact, was a major topic of discussion at the summit. Sixty-three percent of gun deaths are suicides — and suicide is often not thought of by the public as a violence or public health issue, noted experts at the summit. Educating the public about the issues and risk factors can save lives, said Liza Gold, MD, a clinical and forensic psychiatrist and distinguished fellow of the American Psychiatric Association.

However, history suggests health advocates can make a difference. Leadership and collaboration has helped to stem the tide of other public health issues, and during the summit, public health leaders heralded their successes. Samuel "Woodie" Kessel, MD, MPH, former assistant surgeon general and pediatrician, touted successes in other issues that affect children, in particular, as examples for gun safety advocates to emulate.

Lead poisoning reduction, car safety and tobacco use prevention have all been extremely successful in the last decades, Kessel said. Not only are they cause for celebration, they are maps to use now.

"We no longer talk about accidents," Kessel, an APHA member, said. "Accidents are a way of dismissing the issue. We changed it to 'intentional or unintentional injury.' In public health, we talk about identifying risk factors."

RECENT ATTACKS OF GUN VIOLENCE HIT HOME FOR PUBLIC HEALTH WORKERS

APHA reached out to the San Bernardino County Department of Public Health in California in December following a shooting that took the lives of department staff.

On Dec. 2, shooters attacked a health department event at the Inland Regional Center in San Bernardino. Most of the 14 people killed at the center were health department staff who worked on the environmental health services team. APHA Executive Director Georges Benjamin, MD, offered support to the department after the shooting, which he called "senseless."

In a Dec. 4 editorial published online in *The Guardian*, Benjamin called for a public health response to combating the U.S. epidemic of gun violence. Among the measures that should be taken are background checks for all gun purchases and legislation from Congress that would support gun violence prevention research, he said.

"Health epidemics don't end unless we intervene, taking the best science about what does and does not work and using it," Benjamin said. "The epidemic of intentional gun violence can be reversed with a science-based approach."

The San Bernardino shooting came less than a week after a gunman attacked a Planned Parenthood clinic in Colorado Springs, Colorado, killing three people. That incident was "an appalling act of violence" that terrorized health care professionals, according to Vicki Cowart, president and CEO of Planned Parenthood Rocky Mountains.

1. Do you think it makes sense to treat guns as a public health problem? Why might this approach be more effective than bans?

2. Advocates of this approach generally make the comparison between guns and seat belts, tobacco warning labels, etc. Are these fair comparisons?

"KIRBY FERRIS INTERVIEWS AARON ZELMAN," BY KIRBY FERRIS, FROM JEWS FOR THE PRESERVATION OF FIREARMS OWNERSHIP, 2009

Jews for the Preservation of Firearms Ownership recognizes its 20 Anniversary this year. Here is an interview with JPFO's founder Aaron Zelman. Aaron is questioned by contributing writer Kirby Ferris on matters surrounding "Gun Control". This is extracted from the Freedom Flyer PDF files which can be found on the "Freedom Flyer" page.

KF: Socially speaking, what is your original background with firearms?

AARON: I was raised in Tucson, Arizona, where, I like to say, there were more guns than cactuses. Like most rural youths, I fired a .22 when I was ten or twelve. Ironically this was at a Jewish day camp in Tucson! I seriously doubt that this would be happening today, because liberal Judaism has become so widespread. Additionally, one of the nation's experts on ammunition reloading lived across the street from me. I bought my first guns via mail order. Obviously, today's America isn't what I grew up with. Additionally, many in Arizona's Jewish community were the ancestors of pioneers who came to the Southwest in covered wagons. In nearly every photo of the descendents in the book "We Were There" the pioneer Jews are armed. Many of these Jews came from Eastern Europe or Russia and were probably very grateful to finally be on the right end of a gun.

KF: When did you first suspect that American politicians and cultural leaders were beginning to subvert the intent of the Second Amendment?

AARON: It was when the Gun Control Act of 1968 (GCA '68) was passed. How could such an ill conceived, draconian collection of anti-American laws be instituted in a nation founded upon the ideal of an armed citizenry?

KF: So, some twenty years later, in 1989, you decided to form Jews for the Preservation of Firearms Ownership. Why even say "Jews"? Why not "Americans for the Preservation of Firearms Ownership"?

AARON: An unsettling transformation had taken place in the ranks of "gun control" advocates. GCA '68 was the brainchild of Thomas Dodd, who was not Jewish. The political and emotional advocates of GCA '68, like Lyndon Johnson, Ramsey Clark, the Kennedy family, Jesse Jackson and the Martin Luther King family, were not Jewish. But then, somewhere during the expansion of "gun control" in America, liberal Jewish politicians and spokesmen became a disturbingly large percentage of the high profile gun prohibitionists. The myopically, arrogant viewpoints of Charles Schumer and Howard Metzenbaum began to seriously alarm me.

KF: In my conversations over the years, when I mention JPFO by its full name, people are a bit startled, but then so many of them say: "Well, that makes sense, seeing what Jews have historically been through."

AARON: That non Jews seem to comprehend that in greater percentages than Jews, continues to disturb and disappoint me, considering that Jews are commanded to choose self defense. The Jewish religion teaches the absolute responsibility of self defense and the defense of the helpless. I can no longer refer to Jewish gun prohibitionists as innocently misguided, because JPFO has constantly provided them with common sense reasoning and the lessons of history. I now understand that many of them must be latently suicidal and, in many cases, emotionally unstable. They don't trust themselves (because of their repressed anger against humanity) to possess a firearm, and therefore don't trust others who do own guns. As for someone like Charles Schumer, Dianne Feinstein, or Rahm Immanuel? There simply seems to be an evil, authoritarian essence running through their core.

KF: To be fair, aren't there are a growing number of Jews who are waking up to the dangers of so-called "gun control"?

AARON: At this time, I think the answer is yes, albeit a very small percentage. All of us, not just Jews, live in an increasingly dangerous country. But where are the outspoken Jewish advocates of gun ownership in the media, and in American political life? Why aren't prominent Jews as blatantly visible in the defense of the Second Amendment as they were during the civil rights movement, when they marched for "equality"? Disarming honest Americans is a blatant form of inequality.

KF: JPFO came on the scene quite aggressively. Your first ad read: "Not all Jews are stupid or pro criminal, but Charles Schumer is both." And what about your memorable image of Hitler with the headline "All those in favor of "gun control" raise your right hand"? That must have ruffed many feathers throughout the pro "gun control" community.

AARON: But no one has ever stepped forward to intelligently debate us. We didn't publish and publicize that image just to make people upset. JPFO is a solution oriented organization. We reveal the issues, often times with irrefutable historical evidence, and then we offer hard hitting "intellectual ammunition" to combat these well orchestrated and deadly incursions on our liberties.

KF: What will it really take to remove "gun control" from American life?

AARON: There are five crucial steps that must be taken:

1. We must each deeply realize that we have a G-d given right to defend ourselves. It is immoral to interfere with this unalienable, individual right.

2. We must make sure every citizen understands the "Dial 911" hoax. No one has a guaranteed right to police protection.

3. We must make sure that all Americans have a full understanding of the 28 words that make up the Second Amendment.

4. We must demand that politicians explain their reasons for supporting any American law modeled on Nazi policies. Any excuse for such treachery should be political suicide.

5. We must pound home the obvious fact that gun owners will always get the amount of "gun control" they

are willing to tolerate. Gun owners must develop a zero tolerance for "gun control". Otherwise, be prepared to lose a right that was essential to the creation of America.

KF: Are you perhaps talking about making "gun control" politically incorrect?

AARON: Political correctness is poison. Nazis, Communists and Socialists build empires on it. However, what if the psyche of America changed and it became shameful to call someone who was willing to defend their lives, and the lives of the helpless, a "gun nut"? What if it became a cultural taboo, just like calling a Jew or and African-American a derogatory term? All Americans need to realize, that the Charles Schumers and other gun prohibitionists of our country are mentally unbalanced and fear inanimate objects. Should people with this delusional viewpoint be enacting public policies that harm all of us?

KF: So I'll ask you a question that I've been asked. "Do you want everyone armed?"

AARON: Why not? It worked fine for the first 150 years of this nation's history. Anyone who is lawfully adjudicated unfit to carry a firearm should not be on the street in the first place. They should be in prison or in a mental institution. We've thrown the baby (our personal liberties) out with the bathwater, making us helpless to protect ourselves from armed criminals and lunatics. And who promotes this delusional illogic the most fervently? Politicians and the law enforcement hierarchy. Is it only JPFO members who smell this rat?

Even more importantly, JPFO may have been the first organization to point out that governments have murdered far, far more unarmed people throughout history than all the street criminals who ever lived. Statistically, based upon sheer body count, government, any government, is more a threat to your physical safety and life than any number of common street criminals. It's an uncomfortable realization.

KF: Why can't one of the other pro gun organizations do what JPFO is doing?

AARON: When the profile of the gun prohibitionists became blatantly more Jewish, the label of "anti-Semite" was wielded with a heavy hand against those who protested. At that point it became obvious that a Jewish pro gun organization was sorely needed. I've been called a few things in my time, but "anti-Semitic" would be laughable. Historically "gun control" has been a fundamental tool of anti-Semitism. It is also racist and totalitarian, because African Americans were the targets of the first American gun prohibition schemes, and "gun control" preceded every major genocide of the 20th Century.

KF: Has JPFO left its mark? I've had motivated gun owners tell me that JPFO has "radicalized" the entire pro gun movement.

AARON: I believe that JPFO has directed the debate into more fundamental channels. Our moral outrage against the most blatant politicians, our use of educational materials, and our leading edge use technology are matters of pride for me. While the big "pro gun" institution cuddles up to the jack booted goons of the BATFE, JPFO says "Abolish the BATFE". While the big "pro gun" institution says "some gun control is okay", JPFO says "Destroy all 'gun control'. Nothing good can come of it." While the big "pro gun" institution practices "reasonable compromise", JPFO tells the truth: Compromise invites defeat.

KF: Do you think that people are afraid to join JPFO, or any other pro gun group, because they fear they'll be put on a government list?

AARON: That fear is irrational, considering the hard, cold facts. If you have a subscription to a firearms magazine, if you belong to a gun club, if you've ever purchased a hunting or fishing license, if you've ever bought a firearm in a store … and especially if you were ever in the military … you're in the database. If you drive a pickup truck or motorcycle, or have ever ordered anything from a mail order business that also sells hunting and shooting supplies … you are on some government list. Don't be naïve. Based on these inescapable realities, one is working against one's own best interests by not supporting those who are striving diligently to destroy the evil that is "gun control".

KF: Are non Jews invited to join JPFO?

AARON: Absolutely. Anyone who wants to destroy "gun control" will find a home at JPFO. We have never asked the religion of a supporter.

KF: Give me a highlighted retrospective of JPFO projects over the last twenty years, some of the freedom tools that you like to call "intellectual ammunition".

AARON: Before that, I'd like to thank our members. Without their generous and continuing support none of these freedom projects could have ever happened. And, of course, add to this the numerous radio interviews over the years that have brought the JPFO story to the public's attention. In closing I would like to remind people to please access JPFO'S website (www.jpfo.org) search engine to review all the above accomplishments in detail. Then use them to destroy "gun control". If even two or three percent of the probably EIGHTY MILLION gun owners utilized JPFO's material, we would not have "gun control" in America today. Please support our efforts, and tell your friends and family what the members of JPFO have accomplished in our efforts to keep our freedom alive.

1. Do views such as these tend to caricature the gun-control side of the argument? If so, how?

2. Do you think this group is exploiting the Nazi holocaust for political ends, or do you see Nazi Germany as a cautionary tale about what can happen to a disarmed minority?

"WHY THE GUN DEBATE NEVER ENDS," BY TREVOR BURRUS, FROM THE FOUNDATION FOR ECONOMIC EDUCATION, JUNE 28, 2016

It's time for a collective freak-out on guns. It's time to spend too long debating your wife's cousin on Facebook, who seems to have been spoonfed his lines by the NRA/ Everytown for Gun Safety. It's time to unfriend those who keep posting obstinate things about the need for concealed carry/an assault weapons ban. It's time to face-palm about those who just don't get it.

And it is time to just fix the problem, right?

I wish it were that simple, but, like most questions in public policy, it is not. Gun policy is hard, and getting it right—or even starting to get it right—requires calling out the bad arguments from both sides and under-standing inevitable trade-offs and unavoidable facts.

Full disclosure: I'm a gun-rights supporter, insofar as the phrase has a discrete meaning. I've written many pieces arguing for the right to own and carry guns, and against ineffective or uncon-stitutional proposals to curtail gun rights. Yet, with each mass shooting, I grow increasingly despondent about whether any productive debate about guns is happening, much less possible. Consequently, I'm hesitant to write another piece about why mass shootings should not be the focus of gun policy, or about how banning or controlling "assault weapons" should not be the priority of gun-control advocates.

BAD ARGUMENTS FROM GUN-RIGHTS SUPPORTERS

THE OVER-MOTIVATED CRIMINAL

The most common argument offered against new forms of gun control—whether increased background checks, waiting periods, registration, or something else—is that criminals don't follow gun laws. This is true to some degree, and proponents of restrictions acknowledge this, but it goes too far. Every criminal or would-be criminal is not like a Terminator, hell bent on obtaining a firearm to commit a crime. There are marginal, weakly motivated criminals.

Just as there are people who will decide to go elsewhere if Subway raises its prices by twenty cents, there are people who will not acquire a firearm if low-level restrictions are put in their way. Someone who would pay $30 for a Subway sandwich is not affected by a twenty cent increase, and highly motivated criminals are not affected by increased background checks or registration requirements. But there are casual criminals who primarily commit crimes of opportunity that require little effort and entail little risk. Some form of gun control might work by keeping a lethal device out of criminals' hands and curbing their activities.

Oddly, conservatives who make this argument without reservation have historically been the ones arguing that lengthening prison sentences and making punishments more severe would help lower the crime rate. Most adjustments in punishment severity only affect marginal, weakly motivated criminals.

GUNS DON'T CAUSE CRIME, PEOPLE CAUSE CRIME

On one level this is tautologically true. Unlike the scene in James Cameron's *True Lies*, guns don't fall down steps, fire continuously, and magically kill only the bad guys. Except for bizarre and exceptional circumstances, a gun only fires when someone pulls the trigger.

Yet there is a feedback loop between possible criminals and the tools they can obtain. Many people lack the fortitude to commit crimes with a close-up weapon such as a knife or a club. They may want to rob a convenience store, but they'd prefer to do it without getting close to those they threaten. Guns allow those who lack nerve to project immense force over a distance, and therefore, in some sense, guns can cause crime.

The question is what percentage of criminals are like that? If it is only a few, then even somewhat stringent gun-control measures will have only a small effect on the violent crime rate.

THE INEVITABLE SLIPPERY SLOPE TO PROHIBITION

Gun-rights supporters often argue every increase in gun regulation, no matter how tiny, is just one step on the path to the ultimate goal: prohibition. The NRA, in particular, has resisted nearly any gun-control proposal, partially because it warns against the boogey man of prohibition.

Yet, as any philosopher will tell you, a slippery slope is not actually an inevitability. It is always possible to stop. If it weren't, then arguments for more severely punishing criminals would require the death penalty for petty theft. Moreover, gun prohibition is unpopular. Support for banning even one type of gun—handguns—has been declining for decades. Sixty percent of Americans supported banning the private possession of handguns in 1959, compared to only 27 percent today.

CRIMINALS WILL BREAK THE LAWS, SO WHAT'S THE POINT?

Despite the fact that some would-be criminals will certainly be deterred by most gun-control laws (see "The Over-Motivated Criminal") it is true that many will simply break gun laws. Yet that fact is an extremely strange reason for saying that the laws shouldn't exist. Certainly the fact that murderers break laws against murder is not a good argument for repealing laws against murder. Every law is incompletely effective, and some, like speeding laws, might be very ineffective in terms of how many people break them.

The question we must ask instead is whether the costs of a law outweigh its benefits. This is particularly true when it comes to laws concerning guns which, unlike murder, have benefits—whether in the form of subjective pleasure or crime prevention.

IGNORING SUICIDE

Every year, suicide accounts for about two-thirds of gun deaths. While homicide and interpersonal gun violence are the most discussed aspect of gun violence in America, suicide is the most common.

The two issues require different policy approaches, of course. Suicides, like interpersonal gun violence, arise from a constellation of causes, including economic, spiritual and familial. All of these should be discussed, certainly, as well as the prevalence of guns. Guns tend to turn suicide attempts into suicide successes, and many of those people, if they were here today, would regret choosing such an effective method. Gun-control might help this issue, and gun-rights advocates shouldn't ignore the problem.

BAD ARGUMENTS FROM GUN-CONTROL SUPPORTERS

THE UNDER-MOTIVATED CRIMINAL

Just as gun-rights supporters often argue that criminals will overcome any obstacle to get their hands on a weapon, gun-control supporters make the opposite mistake: they imagine criminals as so weakly motivated that procedural obstacles will prevent them from acquiring a gun. As discussed above, the reality is somewhere in between the over-motivated criminal and the under-motivated criminal.

In order to solve this problem, or even begin to understand it, it's crucial to understand the nature of criminals and crime. If most criminals are quite motivated, then gun-control policies enacting mere paper barriers will be quite ineffective.

Moreover, even if guns could be made to disappear, it certainly doesn't mean that motivated criminals wouldn't substitute other methods to accomplish their goals. It might surprise you to learn, for example, that the most common type of robbery in America, 44.5%, is accomplished by using what the FBI calls "strong arm" tactics, threatening to harm the person with your fists or feet. Only 41.6% of robberies are committed with a firearm.

We can infer that criminals willing to commit robbery in such an up-close manner are not generally weakly motivated. Thus, when it comes to robbery at least, gun control may have little to no effect. Moreover, we could see an increase in crime if some people are stripped of the ability to defend themselves.

NOT KNOWING HOW GUNS WORK

Less a bad argument than a rhetorical mistake, gun-control supporters are notorious for not only failing understanding how guns work, but for continuously and, at least to gun-rights supporters, comically, misstating basic facts in public. This lack of understanding is so brazen that gun-rights advocates are rightly concerned that anti-gun politicians simply have no idea what they are talking about.

How bad is it? Really bad. President Obama has said that the Newtown tragedy was committed with a "fully automatic weapon." It wasn't. In fact, automatic weapons—which fire continuously and rapidly for as long as the trigger is pulled and as there are bullets in the magazine—are highly restricted and used in essentially no crimes. Nevertheless, gun-control advocates consistently claim that they are readily available and often used in crime.

Representative Diana Degette (D-CO) once said that bans on high capacity magazines would be effective because the magazines would be unusable after the bullets are gone. This is laughably wrong. There are hundreds of millions of "high capacity" magazines out there and they are refillable. This is about as basic of fact as there is about guns, and that Degette was unaware calls into question her competence to legislate on guns.

Former Rep. Carolyn McCarthy (D-NY) wanted to ban barrel shrouds, but didn't know what they were. The list goes on and on (there are YouTube compilations of the biggest gaffes), and gun-rights supporters are justified in being wary.

THE SLIPPERY SLOPE TO PROHIBITION

Although it is a fallacy for gun-rights advocates to claim that every gun-control measure will lead to confiscation, prohibition or other draconian measures, it is also not unreasonable for gun-rights advocates to be wary of the true goals of some on the other side.

The situation is analogous to abortion. Pro-choice groups are suspicious of attempts by pro-lifers to encumber the right to an abortion with onerous restrictions. Pro-choice advocates understand that the ultimate goal is prohibition, and they thus justifiably resist even small encroachments on a woman's right to choose.

The "Coalition to Stop Gun Violence" was once called the "National Coalition to Ban Handguns. "While it is no longer *en vogue* for politicians and advocacy groups to blatantly argue for prohibition, at one time this rhetoric was quite common. The Coalition to Stop Gun Violence was once called the National Coalition to Ban Handguns, and Handguns Control, Inc. changed its name to the Brady Campaign to Prevent Gun Violence.

Focusing on handguns makes sense. Every year, handguns are used in the vast majority of firearm homicides. But, for seemingly entirely political reasons—i.e. that many people (i.e. voters) now own handguns for self-defense—handguns have become less of a focus in recent years.

In 1979, Sam Fields, then field director of NCBH, insisted that "neither the National Coalition to Ban Handguns, nor any other leading group in the fight for handgun reform, is interested in banning long guns." Yet, by 1990 both NCBH (by then the CSGV) and HCI were campaigning for an "assault weapons" ban. Moves like this make gun-rights supporters inclined to believe that gun-controllers will push for any politically feasible ban on any firearm, even if that means focusing on relatively safe weapons, such as so-called "assault weapons."

Some lawmakers will even admit that "assault weapons" are used in about 2% of gun crimes while still advocating prohibition, leaving gun-rights supporters scratching their heads about why so much political capital is spent on attacking what are arguably the most responsibly owned guns in the country. Meanwhile, other lawmakers have actually admitted that an "assault weapons" ban is "just the beginning."

GUN OWNERS ARE SEXUALLY INADEQUATE PSYCHOPATHS

Many gun control advocates are quite frankly confused by gun owners. That's understandable. Gun ownership is becoming as much a cultural divide as it is a vexing policy issue. Moreover, a Northeast liberal has less in common with a Southern gun hoarder than just guns—they likely watch entirely different TV shows and movies, eat at entirely different restaurants, and read entirely different books.

Many gun control supporters have adopted a sneering attitude toward those who enjoy owning guns. Most typically, gun owners are accused of being sexually inadequate. Often owning a gun is discussed as if it were a symptom of mental disorder. Most recently, in the wake of Newtown, Jim Carrey appeared in a satirical video for the website Funny or Die called "Cold Dead Hand." He lobbed every aspersion on gun owners, focusing particularly on the size of their, um, hands.

Attacks like these help make the chasm between the two sides even wider and decrease the chances that any compromise can ever be reached.

SOME GUNS ARE ONLY GOOD FOR MURDER

For decades, gun-control advocates have singled out particular guns as being "only good for murder." As mentioned above, handguns were once the focus, at least until handguns become more identified with self-defense. Then, so-called "Saturday night specials"—cheap, small caliber handguns often associated with low-income African Americans—became the center of attention, and now we have the current ire over "assault weapons."

Yet, in reality, no popularly owned gun is "only good for killing" or only for "spraying death." The features that make a gun an effective weapon for committing crimes are the same features that make guns effective for self-defense, hunting, sport shooting and target practice. Good guns are reliable, accurate, customizable and powerful enough to accomplish the job, whether it's taking down a deer, a victim or a would-be attacker.

When it comes to the increasingly notorious AR-15, for example, owners appreciate the reliability and customizability. So too do police officers, who often keep AR-15s on hand for the lawful protection of self and others. Unfortunately, some mass shooters also prefer it, but mass shooters are about the most over-motivated criminals around. Take away the AR-15s and other "assault weapons" and they'll find something else.

A gun used responsibly by millions, (including for self-defense), and used by police officers to protect and serve, is simply not a gun only good for murder.

UNAVOIDABLE FACTS AND INEVITABLE TRADE-OFFS

There are plenty of bad arguments to go around, including many I didn't list. Yet all arguments, good or bad, need to be understood within a framework of some unavoidable facts and inevitable trade-offs.

THERE ARE A LOT OF GUNS IN AMERICA, AND THAT'S NOT CHANGING SOON

It is difficult to figure out the exact number of guns in America. There is no gun registry but nearly every estimate places the figure at around 300 million, or about one gun per person. Those guns are not equally distributed, but in general Americans are very well-armed.

Any discussion of gun policy must begin with this fact. Some people believe that, in a civilized society, private citizens would not own guns or that private gun ownership would be heavily regulated. That's fine, but we're not starting from a place where that is a feasible alternative.

Even if confiscation were declared, and 90% of guns were voluntarily turned over to the government—an astounding rate of compliance that defies reasonable belief—there would still be 30 million guns in circulation, which for many gun controllers is still too many.

Those who decide to turn over their weapons would be a particularly civically virtuous bunch. As for those who decide to illegally retain their guns, well, let's just say that we probably wouldn't prefer they are the only ones armed.

SIMPLY ELIMINATING OR HEAVILY REGULATING CERTAIN TYPES OF GUNS WOULDN'T MAGICALLY SOLVE THE PROBLEM, AND IT COULD MAKE IT WORSE

Imagine I give you a magic button and you can eliminate one type of gun. Poof, gone, none left. If you know the stats (see above), then handguns would be the most obvious target.

Yet if handguns were eliminated, that certainly doesn't mean that the approximately 5,500 people likely to be murdered by handguns in the coming year will therefore be saved. Some criminals will substitute other weapons in the place of handguns, mostly knives and "long guns," i.e. rifles and shotguns. This is a problem because long guns are between 1.5-3 times more lethal than handguns.

The next question is how many long guns would be substituted for the now non-existent handguns? Handguns are easily portable and concealable, but a shortened or "sawed off" long gun could be substituted for a handgun in many situations, or the killer could wait for a more opportune time to attack his victim with the weapon available. This is obviously a very difficult question to answer, and guesses range from 30% to as high as 80%.

The net result could mean fewer gunshot victims but more gunshot deaths. If, say, 60% of handgun shooting victims are transformed into long gun shooting victims, then the heightened lethality of long guns could mean that there are actually more total homicides.

The substitution effect is arguably the most vexing problem in gun control policy. It is also the reason why it seems likely that using the magic button to make "assault weapons" vanish would not eliminate mass shooters. I would argue that it wouldn't even put a dent in the number of mass shooters because the proximate reason for a mass shooting rampage is never the presence of a so-called assault weapon.

Mass shooters are highly motivated criminals who will substitute other guns, handguns, hunting rifles, shotguns, etc., to commit their crimes.

PEOPLE DEFEND THEMSELVES WITH GUNS... A LOT

The prevalence of defensive gun use (DGU) is one of the most hotly debated issues in gun control policy. In the words of one study produced by the National Research Council, measuring DGU "has proved to be quite complex, with some estimates suggesting just over 100,000 defensive gun uses per year and others suggesting 2.5 million or more defensive gun uses per year." That's quite a range, but if it falls anywhere in that range then it is still a lot of DGU.

The dispute about the number of DGUs centers primarily on the definition of defensive gun use and the method of counting it. When the Bureau of Justice Statistics performs the National Crime Victimization Survey they ask about DGU, and they generally reach a number around 100,000. Florida State University criminologist Gary Kleck and others have criticized that method because many people are understandably unwilling to tell a government agent that they have brandished or fired a weapon in self-defense. They may not know if what they did was legal, and they may illegally possess the weapon, to name just two concerns. Thus Kleck performed surveys designed to reach just defensive gun use without creating biased concerns in his subjects. Through that method he reached the number 2.5 million.

I'm not going to wade into that debate here (you can read some of my extended commentary), in order to make the basic point that, at least for some people in some circumstances, guns can save their lives. If that ability to protect oneself is removed via a gun control policy, it must be regarded as a cost.

Obviously, the relevant question is whether the only reason some people are defending themselves with guns is because others are attacking them with guns. It's possible that getting rid of the guns would eliminate attackers and thus also eliminate the need for people to defend themselves with a gun. That's only true for those criminals for whom having a gun is what makes them commit crimes, but it is not true for criminals that will attack with knives, clubs and fists.

In that situation, disarming both the attacker and the victim would likely result in more victims because mutual disarmament tends to put the non-violent person at a disadvantage. But those victims would suffer injuries from knives, clubs and fists, which are generally preferable to gun-shots in terms of survivability. Some argue that is what we should be aiming for: a higher crime rate but a lower homicide rate. Perhaps, but any serious discussion of these issues must deal with the difficult trade-offs involved.

For many gun control advocates, the idea that we're supposed to arm ourselves against criminals to the point that everyone is walking around with a gun seems, well, barbaric. And I sympathize. I'd too would rather live in a society where such things aren't necessary; I'm just not sure how to get there because, well, gun policy is hard. In the meantime, I, personally, don't want to disarm people for whom a gun could be a life-saving device. Your mileage may vary.

CONCLUSION

These are just some of the difficulties that arise when trying to do good gun policy. No amount of Facebook meme sharing, congressional sit-ins, or shouting television personalities makes gun policy easier.

Gun policy is hard.

1. Do you agree with this author's analysis of "good" and "bad" gun arguments? Why or why not?

CHAPTER 5

WHAT THE MEDIA SAY

The media tend to polarize opposing viewpoints on guns. Social media posting does this too, but through the "echo chamber" and attendant misinformation characteristic of the Internet. As a result, the gun dialogue has splintered off into hostile camps. Gun rights absolutists denounce the "liberal bias" of media outlets like the *New York Times* and *Washington Post*. Conversely, progressives caricature gun rights defenders as irrational zealots, or "gun-nuts." This too ignores the real legal foundation upon which the right to bear arms rests, however misguided the elevation of this right to a sacred principle might appear to some.

It is against this backdrop that Kurt Eichenwald, writing for *Newsweek*, suggests that each side has something to learn from the other. The right to keep and bear arms is never going away. We must accept this fact without abrogating our responsibility to support measures to ameliorate the public health menace guns have become.

"AMERICANS DON'T HAVE THE RIGHT TO BEAR JUST ANY ARMS; THERE IS AN EASY SOLUTION TO AMERICA'S ARGUMENTS ABOUT GUN CONTROL, BUT THE CHILDISH EXTREMISTS ON BOTH SIDES NEED TO LEAVE THE ROOM," BY KURT EICHENWALD, FROM *NEWSWEEK*, JULY 24, 2015

Let's start with an undeniable truth: In the United States, the people have the right to keep and bear arms. And let's then acknowledge that the childish interpretation of that constitutional amendment—that Americans have the right to whatever accessory they can put on, in or over a gun for the sole purpose of making it more deadly—is a dangerous falsehood.

Therein lies the chasm between those seeking constitutionally impossible forms of gun control and their political opponents, who view every proposal regulating weaponry as the first step toward dictatorship. Caught in the middle are the majority of Americans who think people should be allowed to keep guns but seesaw over tougher laws regarding those weapons.

There is, however, a simple solution, a common-sense compromise that will infuriate both sets of extremists in the gun debate, but would place the United States on a saner path:

- Ban accessories that serve no purpose other than to transform guns into weapons of mass slaughter, such as attachable drums that carry 100 rounds.

- Adopt rules that make it harder for criminals and the mentally ill to obtain firearms.
- Outlaw the public display of weapons.
- Allow the concealed carry of guns using the "shall issue" standard.
- Stop trying to ban scary-looking add-ons that primarily protect the shooter, but don't make the gun more dangerous to others.
- Forget attacks on the "armor-piercing bullets."
- Abandon efforts to outlaw "assault weapons"— a politically loaded phrase with a mishmash of meanings that pretty much amount to nothing.

While any compromise is anathema to the absolutists, it will benefit the rational middle. "Gun control is more analogous to a tourniquet than a Band-Aid," says Osha Gray Davidson, author of *Under Fire*, a history of the National Rifle Association. "Tourniquets save lives, and so will a gun control policy based on balancing rights and responsibilities."

All gun control debates turn on interpretations of the Second Amendment, the worst written and most bizarre part of the Constitution. For example, did you know there are *two* Second Amendments, one passed by Congress and a variation ratified by the states and authenticated by Thomas Jefferson when he was secretary of state? Congress's version—made up of syntactically nonsensical fragments— won the day in the courts, but both versions are grammatical nightmares. Congress's version reads, "A well regulated militia, being necessary to the security of a free State, the right of the people to keep and bear arms shall not be infringed." In the version authenticated by Jefferson, the first comma disappears, transforming the words to a more typical—yet still grammatically confusing—dependent clause followed by an independent clause. That might not sound like much of a difference, but under rules of written English, the words of the amendment used by the courts don't make sense. The confusion has been so great that, in a major Supreme Court case, linguistics professors submitted a brief providing the justices with lessons on the punctuation and grammar.

Throughout the 20th century, that first clause has been argued about endlessly. In a 1939 case, *United States v. Miller*, the Supreme Court held that—because of the opening word fragments of the amendment—the right to weapons (in this case, sawed-off shotguns) had to be read in conjunction with the Militia Clause in Article 1, Section 8. The court wrote, "In the absence of any evidence tending to show that possession or use of a [sawed-off] shotgun—has some reasonable relationship to the preservation or efficiency of a well regulated militia, we cannot say that the Second Amendment guarantees the right to keep and bear such an instrument."

In other words, gun owners in the United States had no right to buy, sell or possess any firearms unless those weapons were reasonably connected to a militia's needs.

That remained the law of the land for decades. That is, until the District of Columbia overreached in 2001, and effectively banned handguns and required owners of firearms to keep them unloaded and disassembled. A lawsuit was filed, the District lost, and it appealed to the Supreme Court. In the landmark 2008 case, *District of Columbia v. Heller,* Justice Antonin Scalia ruled that the first clause of the Second Amendment could essentially be ignored. Despite the critical role those words played in the *Miller* decision, they did not, he argued, qualify the independent clause that followed. Rather, he opined, the words were a "prefatory clause," something akin to a blare of trumpets to declare that a new right was about to be enumerated. "The former does not limit the latter grammatically, but rather announces a purpose," Scalia wrote.

With that, only the independent clause— "the right of the people to keep and bear arms shall not be infringed"—was deemed important. Gun controllers wailed and gun enthusiasts cheered. But that was largely because few of them seemed to have read all of Scalia's opinion. As every first-year law school student knows, constitutional rights are not absolute. Newspapers stay in business thanks to the First Amendment's guarantee of freedom of speech, but they cannot lawfully print child pornography. And citizens have no right to incite imminent violence. Similar restrictions apply to other constitutional rights—most have parameters designed to protect society.

Scalia clearly stated in *Heller* that the right to bear arms had boundaries. "Like most rights, the Second Amendment right is not unlimited," he wrote. "It is not a right to keep and carry any weapon whatsoever in any manner whatsoever and for whatever purpose." For example, he cited laws that prohibit the possession of firearms by felons and the mentally ill, or that forbid them in places such as schools and government buildings, or impose conditions on their sale. He also wrote that his decision did not overrule the holding in the 1939 *Miller* ruling that the sorts of weapons protected are those in common use at the time, and that the "historical tradition of prohibiting the carrying of dangerous and unusual weapons" was still permissible.

In other words, even one of the modern era's most conservative justices says gun enthusiasts are wrong when they claim that any limitation on firearms is unconstitutional. Government can place restrictions on firearms with the intent of protecting society.

Which brings us back to gun accessories. Nowhere in Supreme Court precedent, or in the words of the founders, or in the Second Amendment (either of them) is there a right to attach stuff to a gun, including the add-ons that serve no purpose other than to kill as many people as possible as fast as possible.

Some of these accessories are largely unknown outside of the gun crowd, including such nonsensical devices as magazine drums that allow popular weapons such as the AR-15 rifle to fire up to 100 rounds without reloading.

Why would any gun enthusiast need 100 rounds? James Holmes can tell you. Until July 20, 2012, Holmes was what the NRA would describe as a responsible gun owner. He legally owned a couple of Glock 22 pistols, a Smith & Wesson M&P15 semi-automatic rifle with a 100-round drum magazine, a Remington 870 Express Tactical shotgun, 350 shotgun shells and 6,000 rounds of ammunition. Given all those purchases, his local gun club invited him to join.

Then, on that night in July, Holmes walked into an Aurora, Colorado, movie theater and started firing.

CRITICAL PERSPECTIVES ON GUN CONTROL

He killed 12 people and injured 70 more. He got off 76 shots—65 from the semi-automatic rifle with the 100-round drum; he could have shot more if the drum hadn't jammed. In fact, Holmes told a court psychiatrist that he chose his weaponry in hopes that he would kill all 400 people in the theater.

High-capacity magazines have been the accessory of choice for most mass killers in the U.S. Adam Lanza, the shooter at Sandy Hook Elementary School who killed 20 children and six adults in 2012, used 30-round magazines. The accessory was also used in mass shootings at Columbine High School in 1999 and the military base at Fort Hood, Texas, in 2011.

The Law Center to Prevent Gun Violence reports that half of mass shooters use these magazines. Statistics compiled by the Violence Policy Center in Washington, D.C., show that just in the years Barack Obama has been president, there have been 18 deadly mass shootings involving high-capacity magazines, killing 153 people and wounding 137 more.

A ban on these devices would force a crazed shooter to reload more often, creating more chances for the innocent to get away or even attack the perpetrator. That's how the 2011 mass shooting in Tucson, Arizona, that killed six people and injured 16 others—including Congresswoman Gabrielle Giffords—was stopped: Once the shooter's 33-round magazine was empty, he was tackled while reloading.

Firearms enthusiasts claim these devices are needed because a panicky homeowner, facing armed criminals, would be more likely to miss his target and thus need the extra bullets. Which, of course, is the exact argument against having lots of armed people sitting in a movie theater or at a school ready to fire at a mass shooter: In an emergency, those would-be Rambos are more likely to miss the target and put innocent lives in danger. Rather than wasting money on larger magazines, perhaps gun owners need more target practice.

And no, outlawing these items isn't barred by the Second Amendment. In 2013, Sunnyvale, California, banned high-capacity magazines. The NRA sued in federal court, which—citing *Heller*—ruled these magazines "are hardly crucial for citizens to exercise their right to bear arms." Thus, the court concluded, the potential right to a high-capacity magazine was outweighed—for the same reason the First Amendment doesn't protect bomb threats—by a strong government interest in public safety. An appeals court agreed and the Supreme Court refused to consider the issue further.

The same logic applies to other gun accessories that infringe too greatly on the government's ability to keep citizens safe. Silencers, for example. While they are subject to minimal federal regulation and already banned in 10 states, they are easily obtained and big sellers. There is no reason anyone outside of law enforcement or the military needs one except to kill people without attracting attention. Guns and accessories designed for no rational purpose other than to break the law—such as the weapons that can be made by a 3-D printer with material that won't set off metal detectors—should be forbidden.

Beyond accessories, other changes in gun laws are needed to accomplish what everyone in the debate agrees is a laudable goal: Keep firearms out of the hands of bad guys.

Unfortunately, the NRA has been working for years to make sure lunatics and felons can obtain guns as easily as possible. After the deadliest shooting in American history took place at Virginia Tech (32 dead), Congress passed the NICS Improvement Amendments Act of 2007. When introduced, the legislation called on states to submit mental-health records to national databases maintained by the FBI. The NRA declared this violated the Second Amendment and, through intense lobbying, limited the definition of *mental illness* only to people institutionalized or found by a court to be a danger. Even if a psychiatrist believed a patient posed a threat, nothing could be done to keep a gun out of that person's hand.

Then the NRA worked to weaken old rules barring the mentally ill from owning guns. In the past, because of concerns that an unbalanced person could relapse after treatment, the rules provided that anyone prohibited from having a gun for psychological reasons was banned forever. No more: Now a person committed to a mental hospital can, after getting out, petition a court for his guns. And by lobbying state legislatures, the NRA made sure psychiatric experts play a puny role in determining if a former mental patient should have a gun. Instead, in places like Idaho, state judges who are ill-equipped to make such a determination do it with no input from experts. According to the NRA, every armed madman or criminal is a responsible, law-abiding good guy with a gun until the moment his first bullet splatters the walls with the brains and blood of innocent people.

So ignore the extremists. The only way to keep guns out of the hands of bad guys is to figure out who they are before they get armed. That means universal background checks and record-keeping requirements for all firearms transactions. Under federal law, purchases from a licensed gun dealer require identification, and a form stating the buyer is purchasing it for himself and is not part of a group prohibited from obtaining a gun—felons, people under felony indictment, drug addicts, fugitives and the like. Then, after a background check (90 percent of them take a few minutes), the sale is complete. The dealer makes a record of the transaction and keeps it permanently.

That's a wonderful system, and it is totally worthless in the real world, because almost half of all gun sales are private transactions that entail no procedural safeguards. No identification is required, there's no background check, and no records are kept. This is wonderful for a criminal—or a psychopath. This is what gun opponents mistakenly refer to as the "gun show loophole," but no such loophole exists. Private parties are allowed to sell at gun shows—and anywhere else.

That is why the laws on private sales are absurd. While the NRA "demands" that guns be kept out of the hands of criminals, it has always blocked the only means of doing so: universal background checks on private-party sales. Polls show overwhelming support for checks—as much as 92 percent in a Quinnipiac University poll from last year, including 86 percent of Republicans.

But first the background check process has to be tightened up across the board, as was made obvious in the case of Dylann Roof, the man arrested for the recent shooting spree in an African Methodist Episcopal church in Charleston, South Carolina. Roof obtained a .45-caliber pistol in April from a federally licensed gun dealer but never should have been able to. He was charged in February with possession of a prescription narcotic, which would have prohibited a dealer from selling him a firearm. Under the rules, the government had three days to check out Roof. Because of a mix-up, the Federal Bureau of Investigation was still trying to obtain his arrest record after the three days passed. While national gun dealers won't sell weapons without FBI clearance, smaller stores are less careful. So Roof returned after the three days and, with no completed background check, bought his gun. The lesson? All gun transactions have to use the national chain standards and wait for the FBI's OK.

The last compromise gun advocates should make is based on the words of that conservative hero, Ronald Reagan: "There is no reason why on the street today a citizen should be carrying a loaded weapon." In his statement, issued as governor in May 1967, Reagan was referring to members of the Black Panther Party—Second Amendment absolutists—who walked into the California State House openly carrying rifles to protest a gun control bill.

Reagan's statement—directed at those Black Panthers publicly brandishing their weapons—should be no different when applied to gun zealots walking through a Chili's restaurant in San Antonio carrying long guns. Or the buffoon with an AR-15 loaded with a 100-round drum who last month walked around an

Atlanta airport. Or the nitwit in Gulfport, Mississippi, who menaced shoppers at a Wal-Mart by loading and racking shells into a shotgun a few weeks ago, forcing an evacuation of the store. In all of these states, that near-sociopathic behavior was legal. But how can anyone tell whether these nincompoops parading around with their guns on display are merely acting like a 4-year-old proudly showing everyone his penis or constitute a deadly menace? Ask someone at the posh Omni Austin Hotel in Texas; earlier this month, a man walked around the lobby with a rifle, legally scaring people. Then he shot and killed someone.

In this great compromise, that is all the gun controllers get: a ban on high-capacity magazines and other slaughter accessories, universal background checks and a ban on the public display of weapons. That brings us to what gun enthusiasts should receive in the bargain.

First, anyone who wants to obtain a license to carry a concealed weapon should be given one. All states *allow* for concealed carry, but many states—like California, New Jersey and Maryland—have what are called "may issue" statutes, meaning people who qualify for a license might not be allowed to receive one. In some states, it's up to county officials to decide who gets to carry a gun inside his or her coat. Here's reality: A criminal or disturbed person will carry a concealed weapon, licensed or not. Under the universal background check system, anyone walking into a state office seeking a concealed carry permit has already been screened; there's no reason to deny that person a license if he or she meets the additional requirements.

Then there are the gun accessories that have spooky names, but are mostly designed to protect the shooter. For example, flash suppressors have been outlawed on the belief they will be used to minimize the chance of spotting a shooter. That is a consequence of the device, not its purpose. In truth, the main reason flash suppressors exist is to disburse burning gases that exit the muzzle of a long-arm gun; this minimizes the chance that the shooter will be blinded in low-light environments. Danger to the public from this accessory: none.

Other accessories also pose minimal danger, and they protect or help gun owners. For example, the barrel shroud and the folding stock were banned in 1994, then legalized in 2003. Gun control advocates have been pushing for them to be declared illegal once again. The reasons are silly. The shroud cools the barrel of the gun, making sure it does not overheat during rapid firing. It is scary looking but doesn't pose any realistic threat. A folding or collapsing stock is used on a long gun and makes it easier to store or transport the weapon. These were outlawed out of a fear that killers would be able to hide their rifles; again, not a reasonable consideration in a world filled with semi-automatic pistols.

It's also time to end this nonsense about "cop killer bullets." Although this topic has been debated since the late 1980s, there is still no accepted definition for this ammo. Earlier this year, though, the Bureau of Alcohol, Tobacco, Firearms and Explosives proposed banning armor-piercing 5.56-millimeter M855 "green tip" rifle rounds as cop killers. Some gun owners use this bullet in big, heavy AR-15 pistols, so ATF decided that the M855 green tip posed a threat to police officers who wear body armor. Problem is, not only is this exceptionally popular rifle ammunition, but ATF can point to no instance in which an officer was shot through body armor by an M855. Faced with outrage by gun owners, ATF dropped the proposal. It should stay dropped.

And so should efforts to ban assault weapons. One fact few gun opponents seem to know: Assault weapons don't exist. There are assault rifles, but the broader category of weapons that were banned in 1994 and legalized in 2003 are a political construct. Again, many of them look scary because of the cosmetic features added by gun manufacturers. But the only thing that makes them more dangerous than any other weapon is the number of bullets they can shoo—an issue dealt with by a ban on high-capacity magazines. A 2004 report for the Justice Department showed that, prior to the ban, the firearms defined as "assault weapons" were used in as few as 2 percent and no more than 8 percent of all gun crimes; almost none of those cases involved assault rifles. However, high-capacity magazines accounted for between 14 percent and 26 percent of all gun crimes. In other words, when it comes to assault weapons, Americans should stop worrying about the guns and pay attention to the bullets.

There it is: a series of reasonable proposals with something to hate for everyone. But extremists on both sides will never get what they want—all guns everywhere or no guns anywhere. It is up to the rational middle—the vast majority of Americans—to tell the fanatics that the grown-ups are taking over.

1. Is this an accurate summation of the gun debate's polarities, in your view?

2. Do you find Justice Scalia's reading of the Second Amendment helpful? Why or why not?

"MEDIA SILENCE ON AN IRATE GUN COMPANY'S CONNECTION TO SANDY HOOK: HOW IS ADAM LANZA NOT PART OF THIS STORY?" BY JASON SALZMAN, FROM *OTHERWORDS*, JANUARY 29, 2014

A Colorado gun-accessories company garnered national media coverage when it announced plans to move most of its manufacturing and sales operations to Wyoming and Texas.

The reports highlighted that the company was pulling up stakes to protest the state's new gun safety laws, which Colorado passed last year.

What did the coverage leave out? The fact that the company, Magpul Industries, manufactured the magazine shooter Adam Lanza used when he gunned down kids and adults in the Newtown, Connecticut massacre.

Over the past year here in Colorado, Magpul has taken a leadership role in opposing gun-safety legislation. Among other things, my state has banned magazines holding 30 bullets, like the one used at Sandy Hook.

During the gun-safety debate in the Colorado Legislature, Magpul threatened to take its 200 jobs and flee Colorado if gun-safety laws were put in place.

The company's executives testified at the same legislative hearings as Jean Dougherty, sister of the slain Newtown psychologist Mary Sherlach. Colorado Republican lawmakers, meanwhile, helped set up Magpul as the face of Democratic "over-reach" on the gun legislation. Those state legislators said this legislation was unpopular, even though polls showed otherwise.

The Republican State Senate leader scolded Democrats for backing legislation that would drive away the company. He pointed out that Magpul magazines were used by Navy Seals in their killing of Osama bin Laden.

At the time, it wasn't known that a Magpul magazine was also used at Newtown, even though the chances were good, because Magpul makes the most popular brand of 30-round magazine sold nationwide.

After a law limiting magazines sold in Colorado to holding 15 bullets or fewer, Magpul stepped up its political activities, leading a major fundraising event for the recall campaigns against two Democratic State Senators who voted for the new gun laws.

At one fundraiser, the company sold over 15,000 magazines for $10 each, with all the money from sales going toward the recall effort. Eventually, both lawmakers were voted out of office in the recall election.

It was a highly unusual political ride for a private company, especially one with such an obvious vested interest in the outcome. Obviously, companies get involved in politics, especially on the money side, but to take such a high-profile lobbying position at the state level, including involving itself in a recall campaign? That's rare, if not unprecedented.

But things turned sour for Magpul at the end of last year, when Connecticut police reported that a Magpul magazine was used at Sandy Hook.

Magpul's response? Silence.

After rushing to every microphone in Colorado during the legislative battle, Magpul had nothing to say to reporters about its connection to the Newtown shooting, even when photos of its magazines, used by the shooter, were released in December.

Then, Magpul jumped back into the news last week, when it announced its departure from Colorado.

But even though the company was exacting revenge for a gun law that might have prevented a gunman from having a 30-round magazine had it been in place in Connecticut or nationally, reporters didn't mention that Magpul's bullet holders were used at Sandy Hook.

To be fair, journalists could have mentioned that the U.S. military uses Magpul magazines against our enemies, as well as the fact that mass murderers use them at home.

How is this information not an integral part of the Magpul story?

1. What information could be left out from media reports about gun violence? Why?

"THINK GAYS DON'T NEED GUN RIGHTS? CHECK YOUR PRIVILEGE," BY CATHY REISENWITZ, FROM THE FOUNDATION FOR ECONOMIC EDUCATION, JUNE 28, 2016

A predictable response to the horrific massacre at a gay nightclub in Orlando, in which a gunman murdered 49 people and injured 53 others, mostly Latino, is to restrict gun ownership to police only.

But this response ignores the real relationship gay and ethnic minority populations have had with police. It's a history of violence, targeted specifically at queer and brown bodies.

When we discuss privilege in America, we rightly point out that straight, white, cisgendered, male Americans have the tremendous advantage of not being directly negatively impacted by institutional, systemic racism, sexism, transphobia and homophobia.

But what we don't discuss often enough is how American law enforcement privileges the lives of straight, white, cisgendered, male Americans over the lives of others.

Those who dream of a utopia in which only the police have guns must reckon with the reality that to disarm everyone but the police puts marginalized communities at the utter mercy of American police departments who have proven themselves to be more than happy to violate black and queer bodies, and court systems which have proven themselves unwilling to hold them accountable.

A HISTORY OF RACIAL VIOLENCE

Despite what you've been taught, the fight for equality under the law for black Americans did not start with boycotts and marches. It started with black guys with guns.

Most Americans immediately connect Reverend Martin Luther King Jr. and Rosa Parks to the civil rights movement. You probably also know Emmett Till. But you may not know Dr. T. R. M. Howard.

Emmett Till was the third black male to be murdered in Mississippi in a three-month span 1955.

After trying to vote in Belzoni, Reverend George Lee was shot and killed at point blank range while driving. Weeks later Lamar Smith succeeded in casting his ballot in Brookhaven before he was shot and killed in broad daylight, before witnesses in front of the county courthouse.

Police made no arrests in connection to either murder. Witnesses rightly feared for their lives and did not come forward to testify.

Then on August 28, 1955 three men kidnapped 14-year-old Emmett Till at gunpoint around 2 a.m. They put Till in the bed of a pickup truck and drove him to various places to pistol whip him and decide what to do. Finally they shot him dead. Before dumping his body, the murderers showed his mutilated corpse to a black man saying, "That's what happens to smart niggers."

Till's crime wasn't voting, but whistling. A habit he picked up to alleviate his stuttering, a few white men thought it was directed at a white girl.

Till's mother, Mamie Till Bradley, insisted on an open-casket viewing of Till's mutilated body and tens of thousands of people showed up to see it. Till's murder and the sight of his body enraged and activated civil rights leaders at the state and national levels of the NAACP. But everyone still feared for their lives too much to come forward and testify.

That's when wealthy physician and civil rights leader Dr. T. R. M. Howard came forward. Howard used his considerable wealth to hire armed bodyguards to protect himself, his family, and anyone else willing to come forward to testify against Till's murderers.

These witnesses made the trial possible, and the trial was "The first great media event of the civil rights movement," according to the *New York Times*.

While Till's murderers were acquitted, the tide had turned. Armed black people were no longer too afraid to stand up about injustice. Howard made sure Mose Wright, the first man to ever testify against a white man in court and live, was able to escape to Chicago after the trial.

Two months after Till's murder, Montgomery civil rights activists held a meeting to discuss Till's case and other recent murders of civil right activists. Rosa Parks attended this meeting, and then one month later she refused to give up her seat to a white passenger on a Montgomery city bus.

POLICE VIOLENCE AGAINST QUEER AMERICANS

The story of the struggle for gay rights has been similarly sanitized.

Black Americans in the south could not rely on law enforcement for help. In the leadup to the Till trial, Tallahatchie County Sheriff Clarence Strider told the media he believed Till's body was not Till's but was a decoy planted by the NAACP. He confined two witnesses to jail to prevent them from testifying. And during the trial he said to black spectators coming back from lunch, "Hello, Niggers!"

The relationship between queer Americans and law enforcement is even worse.

Rampant homophobia and transphobia in the 1960's meant out queers were unwelcome in most bars and restaurants. That made the places they were allowed extremely important. But it also made them a target for police raids. States adopted anti-sodomy legislation for the purpose of giving police a pretext for mass arrests of queers. By 1960, every state had an anti-sodomy law.

In New York, the gay bars were mostly controlled by organized crime who paid off police to prevent frequent raids. Yet the raids were still pretty frequent, happening once per month for each bar on average. San Francisco gays had it no better. When police showed up to Compton's Cafeteria to arrest men dressed as women in 1966. This time, the patrons rioted, slinging cups and plates and breaking the plexiglass windows.

When police conducted an unannounced raid at the Stonewall Inn, a mafia-owned gay bar in Greenwich Village, patrons and supporters rioted violently for days. This inspired organized meeting and marches for gay rights. Before two years had passed after the Stonewall riots every major American city had a gay rights group.

THE DISTURBING REALITY

It would be lovely if equality under the law were a reality in America today. But you only have to look as far as the murders of Freddie Gray or Eric Garner to see that we are not there yet.

Here's what the Baltimore Police Department tweeted after one of their officers was acquitted in the death of Freddie Gray. [*Editor's Note: The tweet shows Leonardo DiCaprio in the film* The Great Gatsby *holding up a glass of wine, with the caption "Here's to the Baltimore 6 Defense Team, the FOP and Detective Taylor.*]

They raised a toast to the fact that the officer who decided not to put a seatbelt on the handcuffed Freddie Gray and drove him around the city, every twist and turn throwing his body against the metal walls, whose actions are directly responsible for his untimely, violent death, would face no criminal penalties.

Gun control puts marginalized Americans at the utter mercy of a police force that has perpetrated thousands of violent raids of gay nightclubs, yet could do absolutely nothing to stop the massacre in Orlando. Gays need guns, not only to protect themselves from cops, but also to protect themselves from being targeted by civilians like the Orlando shooter and the homophobes who threatened Tom Palmer.

The people who posit gun control for the purpose of protecting gays in the wake of the Orlando massacre benefit from tremendous privilege. They get to live in ignorance of the role police have played in hurting gay Americans, and in ignorance of the role guns have played in fomenting the movement for civil rights. And in particular, white, straight pro-gun control liberals can safely advocate for disarming the marginalized while they enjoy the privilege of not being heavily targeted by violent bigots, including cops.

Perhaps it's within the realm of possibility that disarming people will protect the marginalized. But only if we disarm the police.

1. This author uses an argument not often used, combing progressive interest in civil rights with the typically conservative interest in gun rights. Is her argument convincing? Why or why not?

CHAPTER 6

WHAT ORDINARY PEOPLE SAY

Recent Gallup polling suggests that Americans are in favor of Congress passing laws requiring more rigorous and extensive criminal and mental health background checks, and also closing the so-called "gunshow loopholes" which allow anyone to purchase a firearm privately, without any background check or dealer licensure requirements.

Possibly due to the inherent difficulty of enforcing such laws, polling also registers low expectations that these measures will prove effective: a majority of poll respondents believe that gun control laws will have little to no effect on the frequency of mass shootings.

If this is the case, should lawmakers focus instead on increasing funding for mental health care, the reduction of poverty, and other approaches to healing a violent and ill society? Why expend scarce political capital on gun control laws when most Americans believe they'll ultimate prove ineffectual anyhow?

Perhaps the answer to this question lies less in outcomes than in the type of society we wish to foster. As Firmin DeBrabander reports below, we've become a "shoot first" society, with "stand your ground" laws providing the legal cover to execute a stranger based on fear and suspicion, rather than an actual threat. More often than not, this perceived threat has a racial dimension. In an alienated, fearful society, more guns feed this vicious cycle. DeBrabander roots his critique of gun rights within the Catholic social gospel, providing a much-needed corrective to a largely pro-gun mainstream Christianity.

"AMERICAN PUBLIC OPINION AND GUNS," BY FRANK NEWPORT, FROM GALLUP.COM, DECEMBER 4, 2015

After the horrific mass shooting in California on Wednesday that resulted in 14 victims being killed, President Barack Obama called again for new gun control measures, saying, "There are some steps we could take not to eliminate every one of these mass shootings, but to improve the odds that they don't happen as frequently: common-sense gun safety laws, stronger background checks." Presidential candidate Bernie Sanders weighed in, saying, "We need to significantly expand

and improve background checks." Hillary Clinton said in Florida, "33,000 Americans a year die. It is time for us to say we are going to have comprehensive background checks, we are gonna close the gun show loopholes."

The American public agrees in principle with these types of proposals. In Gallup's latest October update, 55% of Americans said they supported stricter gun control laws. That 55% is higher than has been typical in recent years, most likely because the poll was conducted shortly after nine people were killed in an Oregon community college mass shooting. But we also found a spike in the desire for stricter gun laws after previous shootings, and no doubt the sentiment is as high or higher now after the California shootings.

More directly, over time, almost any question that we or other pollsters ask Americans about background check laws and other ways of restricting access to guns gets very high support levels. In the October poll, 86% of Americans favored "a law which would require universal background checks for all gun purchases in the U.S. using a centralized database across all 50 states." A recent Quinnipiac poll found 77% support for banning gun sales to those on terrorist watch lists -- a measure proposed by a number of Democratic senators in the last several days. Prior Gallup polling has found strong support for increasing penalties for those who buy guns for others who have not passed background checks, banning the possession of armor-piercing bullets, requiring background checks for those purchasing guns at gun shows, and restricting purchase of high-capacity ammunition clips.

Americans, in short, would be totally on board if Congress were to pass more restrictive background check laws.

But the American public, at the same time, appears doubtful that these background checks would have a major impact on reducing mass shootings -- something Obama recognized when he said that his proposals would not eliminate every one of the mass shootings. Just after most Americans in the October poll said that they approved of a background check law, they were asked to indicate how much this type of new law would reduce the number of mass shootings in the U.S. A majority (53%) of Americans said they thought the law would reduce mass shootings a little or not at all. Just 19% said these laws would reduce the number of mass shootings a great deal and 28% said a moderate amount.

This lack of perceived efficacy of the laws fits with reports showing that California already had strict gun control laws in place. One of the alleged shooters in this situation was born in the U.S. and apparently, from what is known at this point, had little trouble acquiring the weapons even with the background checks and restrictions -- although it is possible that some of the weapons could have been purchased in an adjoining state with less strict laws.

Another alternative would be to ban weapons altogether. Americans do not generally support laws that totally ban anything. In October, only 27% favored a law banning handguns altogether except for law enforcement. Gallup has asked that question for 57 years, and only once -- when it was first asked in 1959 -- did a majority support banning handguns. In 2012, we found 44% of Americans favored a law that would make it illegal to manufacture, sell or possess semi-automatic guns known as assault rifles, while 51% opposed. Prior to that, however, in 1996 and 2000, this measure found majority support. When phrased differently in a 2013 poll, 56% of Americans said they would vote for a law that would reinstate and strengthen the ban on assault weapons that was in place from 1994 to 2004 -- the higher level of support perhaps resulting from the fact that the question reminded respondents that this law had been on the books previously.

The October poll did give us an indication that more Americans are now concerned enough about guns and gun control to say that it would affect their propensity to vote for certain candidates. The 26% of registered voters who said they would only vote for a candidate who shares their views on gun control is considerably higher than what we found when we asked the same question in 1999 and 2000. This sentiment is more likely to be held by those who are opposed to stricter gun control than those who support it. Conservatives are also more likely than liberals to say they would take a candidate's position on guns into account.

News reports indicate that gun sales may have soared over the Thanksgiving Day weekend, based on data showing a big increase in FBI background checks. The apparent uptick in gun sales could be driven by Americans' desire to have guns for protection. In fact, the October Gallup poll showed that a majority of Americans think the nation would be safer if more Americans carried concealed weapons. A different trend question asked in 2014 found that Americans believe having a gun in the house makes it safer rather than more dangerous -- a marked shift in opinion from previous polling. A Pew Research poll similarly found that a majority of Americans believe owning guns does more to protect people from being the victim of crime that put them at risk.

Where does that leave elected officials who understandably are looking for ways to help reduce the mass shootings that have so tragically dominated the news in recent years? Research shows that the lawmakers' constituents, taken as a collective whole, believe the Second Amendment was designed to give the public the right to bear arms. Nearly 70% of Americans have shot a gun in their lifetime, and more than four in 10 have a gun in their home, suggesting that guns are, to some degree, a way of life in America. The public resists outright bans on owning guns, although they support many different proposals to restrict ownership and have been willing to countenance the idea of a ban on assault weapons in the past. The majority believe that more Americans owning concealed weapons would make the nation safer rather than more dangerous.

The idea of passing new gun laws has the appeal of representing straightforward, concrete action. Americans are all in favor of their lawmakers passing more laws restricting access to guns, although -- and this is key -- Americans are not convinced that such laws are going to be highly effective in reducing mass shootings.

A more complex approach is to attempt to understand why it is that shooters engage in mass shootings, and what it is about society and culture today that may provide the context in which individuals make decisions to engage in such catastrophic, deadly behaviors -- and then to attempt to address those causes. But, as is true with the attempt to understand a lot about human behavior, it is very hard to isolate these types of factors, which can range across focus points such as youthful alienation, religious fundamentalism, terrorist organizations, mental instability, the lack of meaning in young people's lives, the lack of jobs, the loss of personal identity, peer relations, copycat behaviors and so forth. Even if these types of causes can be determined, it is obviously going to be very difficult to implement simple or timely steps that would change them.

1. According to this poll, Americans support laws restricting access to firearms, but remain skeptical that these laws will be very effective in preventing mass shootings. Do you agree with this general feeling?
2. This summary claims that Americans do not support a ban on anything. Can you think of any exceptions to this generality?

"OUR ARMED SOCIETY: THE COMMON GOOD IS THE FIRST VICTIM OF AMERICA'S GUN CULTURE," BY FIRMIN DEBRABANDER, FROM *AMERICA*, SEPTEMBER 14, 2015

Among the so-called advanced societies of the world, only in the United States are there regular scenes of gun violence and suffering like that witnessed in July in Lafayette, La., after an apparently unbalanced middle-aged man fired off 20 rounds in a movie theater, killing two and injuring nine, or like the even more devastating spectacle that engulfed Charleston, S.C., the month before that when a hate-filled young man began a murderous rampage inside a historic African-American church, killing nine people during a Bible study.

And in the month just before that in Waco, Tex., on May 17, a dispute among biker gangs erupted into an epic gun battle outside a chain restaurant in a suburban shopping center. A witness likened it to a war zone, with "maybe 30 guns being fired in the parking lot, maybe 100 rounds"; families with small children were forced to scatter for cover. In the end, that violence left nine people dead and 18 injured. Authorities collected more than 100 guns from the brawling bikers. Amid reports of other bikers pouring in to Waco to take up the battle, the city was locked down. People were afraid to leave their homes.

This is what passes for normal life in our armed society--enjoying the "freedom" that the National Rifle

Association promises as the number of civilian firearms in the United States soars and easy access to guns continues. The gun rights movement has made sure of this. The N.R.A. has fought universal background checks for prospective buyers and uses its political power to limit the ability of the Bureau of Alcohol, Tobacco and Firearms to regulate gun dealers and track illegal guns and guns used in crimes.

The gun rights movement's solution to gun violence is more guns—always more guns. Its supporters argue that we must ensure that the "good guys" among us are well armed, as Wayne LaPierre, executive vice president and chief executive officer of the N.R.A., memorably put it, and we must expand the number of public venues where guns can be legally carried. After the 2012 shooting at Sandy Hook Elementary School in Newtown, Conn., where 20 first-graders were killed, the N.R.A. recommended placing armed guards in every school in the nation and training and arming teachers and staff. Many school districts obliged.

Since the shooting in 2007 at Virginia Tech, where a gunman killed 32 people, the gun rights movement has persuaded legislators in nine states to allow students and faculty with appropriate permits to carry their weapons on public university campuses. Ten more states are considering similar legislation this year. It seems the very notion of gun-free zones is endangered. In April 2014 Georgia passed a controversial law—a so-called guns-everywhere statute—allowing residents to bring firearms into bars and restaurants, airports and government buildings.

THE 'SHOOT FIRST' SOCIETY

In a lesser known and heralded policy position, the U.S. Conference of Catholic Bishops has called for stronger gun control. The bishops released an impassioned plea to lawmakers shortly after Sandy Hook, urging them to support bills that would make guns safer and restrict easy access to firearms. But American Catholics have not embraced gun control as a central tenet of their parish social justice agendas. This must change.

The gun rights ideology, which says we need ever more guns to deal with the threat of violence, that we must expand the number of public places where people may carry weapons and that we must legally protect people who use firearms, is opposed to the message of the Gospel and Catholic social teaching. The radical agenda of the contemporary gun rights movement undermines the very basis of civil society, reducing community members to atomistic, alienated individuals and contradicts the Catholic doctrine of the common good.

The gun rights movement is busy creating a shoot-first society. This is the upshot of so-called stand-your-ground legislation, now on the books in more than 20 states. Stand your ground is the logical, legalistic extension of our armed society; it effectively emboldens gun owners to use their weapons in public. Indeed, what good is owning and carrying a gun for self-protection if you are not also legally protected in using it?

Stand your ground was invoked in the case of the retired police officer Curtis Reeves after he shot an unarmed man he argued with in a Tampa movie theater in January 2014. The victim had allegedly thrown popcorn in Reeves's face. His lawyer said Reeves did not know his assailant's only weapon was popcorn; in the darkened theater, he feared his opponent was better armed.

Fair enough. In a stand-your-ground society, it makes sense to suspect and fear your neighbor. You do not know what weapons he may have, how he might use them and over what complaint, no matter how trifling. What if he decides, like George Zimmerman, who in 2012 confronted and killed an unarmed teenager, Trayvon Martin, that you look suspicious, and he picks a fight with you? The law effectively can offer legal cover to shooters who, fearing for their personal safety, feel justified in using deadly force in self-defense. Ironically, of course, that is precisely the feeling they are more likely to have thanks to stand-your-ground ordinances.

The armed society obstructs our ability to fulfill the church's teaching and work for the common good, a foundational concept in Catholic social teaching. St. Thomas Aquinas affirmed that we are political by nature and that the aim of the political community is to advance this common good. The personal success and welfare of each individual is bound up with it, and people cannot hope to advance individual goals without accepting and contributing to it; but the common good is not the mere accumulation of individual goods. As the *Compendium of the Social Doctrine of the Church* puts it: "The human person cannot find fulfillment in himself apart from the fact that he exists 'with' others and 'for' others. This truth does not simply require that he live with others at various levels of social life, but that he seek unceasingly--in actual practice the good found in existing forms of social life."

Cooperation and interaction are necessary conditions of this social life, the compendium affirms. But stand-your-ground laws drive people apart; they sow and then validate mutual mistrust.

America's profusion of arms makes us instinctively wary of reaching out to others, even in acts of charity. It becomes impossible to "seek the good of others as though it were one's own good," as the church urges, because an armed society opposes the primary and requisite identification with others. In a stand-your-ground world, other people are a source of fear--a source of danger. I have to worry about even minor misunderstandings, should my actions and outreach be interpreted as a threat.

A DEADLY FORCE

Busy making guns a fixture in public spaces, the gun rights movement ironically compels a radical retreat from the public sphere. Guns are inherently isolating. A gun indeed communicates; it communicates a threat. This is its nature, and gun rights proponents admit as much when they proudly assert that the weapon on one's hip serves as a warning—a warning of deadly force.

This is a disincentive to look for Christ in others, as the Gospel urges us to do—as Jesus' disciples discovered on the road to Emmaus, when they invited a stranger to dinner and discovered he was the risen Christ. Jesus tells us that we encounter him in others when we reach out to them and serve them, when we extend the bonds of love. Jesus is found precisely in a rich, open public life. What is more, he urges us to reach out to those we would be least inclined to engage because we fear them or disdain them, or suspect them. "Whatever you did for one of these least brothers of mine, you did for me," Jesus tells us.

A favorite saying of the gun rights movement is that "an armed society is a polite society." That is, guns sprinkled liberally throughout a community will effectively scare people straight. People will behave lest they insult or offend gun owners, and God help any prospective criminals. But I imagine it otherwise: an armed society is distinctly uncomfortable, treacherous and electric. The gun rights recipe for peace sounds more like a constant tense and tenuous standoff between warring parties. It is no prescription for lasting social peace and security.

Guns by their nature frustrate discourse; they chasten speech. If you should spy an armed citizen on a street corner, you are not more likely to walk up to greet him unannounced, but less so. Most people will hurry the other way. Gun rights proponents will object at this point, saying that if or when guns are a regular feature of everyday life--in other words, a commonplace--they will not hinder conversation. Perhaps. But this does not change the fact that guns certainly do not invite conversation and interpersonal contact. Guns are mutually alienating.

The theologian Jacques Maritain suggested how an armed society violates natural law. "Each one of us has need of others for his material, intellectual and moral life," Maritain explained in *The Rights of Man and Natural*

Law, "but also because of the radical generosity inscribed within the very being of the person, because of that open-ness to the communications of intelligence and love which is the nature of the spirit and which demands an entrance into relationship with other persons." Of our nature, we are outwardly directed, driven and disposed. We cannot live without others; we require their contribution and interac-tion. On our own, we are incomplete. The church teaches that we must work in and with a political community advancing the common good in order to perfect our nature.

Mr. LaPierre declares that supporting the gun lobby's agenda "is a massive declaration of individual rights." To be sure, gun-rights absolutism demands nothing short of radical individualism, sliding into a dangerous and foolhardy, and ultimately destructive, insistence upon self-determination and self-suffi-ciency. Mr. LaPierre is prone to listing the many hostile forces that oppose individuals in society, beginning with the government, which "can't or won't, protect you.... Only you can protect you!" To gun owners, he declares, "We are on our own!"

SEEKING SECURITY

But an individual cannot ensure his security on his own for long. Real security rests on the integrity of society at large, which is contingent on the cooperation of others and, in a democracy, the rule of law. The N.R.A. touts gun ownership as the best way to protect your private property, your person and your family. But in a society without the rule of law and its recognition by others, your property is hopelessly imperiled, no matter how great your arsenal.

The gun rights movement willfully, at times happily, ignores the rule of law, but the rule of law is what ensures the seamless functioning of modern democratic societies. Everyone can go about their business because they assume their neighbors recognize and respect the rule of law. They share the conviction that invisible, tacitly accepted and understood laws govern society and that everyone will behave accordingly and predictably. If, by contrast, good behavior must be ensured at the barrel of a gun, as gun rights proponents maintain, then all bets are off; I can assume nothing about anyone else's behavior. Needless to say, it fundamentally changes my everyday life and makes it impossible to pursue ordinary business.

"In the world that surrounds us," Mr. LaPierre told the 2014 Conservative Political Action Committee convention, "there are terrorists and home invaders and drug cartels and car-jackers and knock-out gamers and rapers [sic], haters, campus killers, airport killers, shopping mall killers, road rage killers, and killers who scheme to destroy our country with massive storms of violence against our power grids, or vicious waves of chemicals or disease that could collapse the society that sustains us all." The implication is clear: The rule of law is quite nearly vanished; civil society is on the brink, if not already destroyed in parts of the country.

These are no harmless, idle pronouncements. In the hands of the gun rights movement, they become a self-fulfilling prophecy. A proliferation of guns in society, increasingly prevalent in public spaces and used in stand-your-ground states to neutralize imagined threats, undermines the conviction that the rule of law still pertains. People who have no gun start to think they too should be armed--and ready to use their weapon. That erodes the rule of law even more. In short, the gun rights movement creates the world it warns us of—where differences are decided by gunfire, as in Waco.

To that extent, Mr. LaPierre gives up on humanity; he would reduce us to our mere physical being, engrossed in selfish, material concerns. "In this uncertain world, surrounded by lies and corruption," he told the crowd at the convention, "there is no greater freedom than the right to survive, to protect our families with all the rifles, shotguns and handguns we want."

The church maintains far higher aspirations. "The human being is a person, not just an individual," the compendium tells us, and "does not find complete self-fulfillment until he moves beyond the mentality of needs and enters into that of gratuitousness and gift, which fully corresponds to his essence and community vocation."

Political society is not an end in itself, according to the church. We have a higher destiny, an ultimate end in Christ. But we cannot hope to attain that end, Aquinas knew well, unless we inhabit a society that promotes the fullest development of the human person in all its capacities and encourages and makes possible outreach and service.

We require such personal preparation to invite grace, and this is achieved in a political society devoted to pursuing the common good. The common good demands that we resist the radical agenda of the gun rights movement and work to bring peace to this armed society.

1. This piece argues against guns from a religious (Catholic) angle. Meanwhile, the Christian Right—who typically support gun rights—espouses very different beliefs. How might we reconcile this disagreement? Which side do you support?

2. The author claims that the "gun rights movement willfully, at times happily, ignores the rule of law." Is this accurate?

"COMMON SENSE: IT'S TIME FOR POLICE OFFICERS TO START DEMANDING GUN LAWS THAT COULD END UP SAVING THEIR OWN LIVES," BY ROBERT WILSON, FROM *THE AMERICAN SCHOLAR*, 2016

When we send our soldiers, spies, and mercenaries into dangerous situations, we have and should have high expectations for how they will behave. Murder, rape, and pillage—the dark acts of soldiery in wartime—are heinous crimes even when our own soldiers commit them, and lesser acts of cruelty and destruction are also intolerable. Although it would be naive to think that we prosecute more than a fraction of such crimes, that we prosecute them at all speaks to our values and to the standards we have for the behavior of our soldiers. Still, if we are honest about what war is and what can reasonably be expected of those we expose to the boredom, tension, and danger of combat, then we know that criminal acts are inevitable, and that when we send people to kill our enemies, innocent people will also die or be exposed to horrible injury or loss. Those who commit the felonies and misdemeanors of war are of course responsible for them, and deserve to be condemned and punished. But the rest of us who are not exposed to danger can't wash our hands of the consequences or profess to be shocked when shocking crimes are committed under the pressures of soldiering.

In the past two or three decades, we have increasingly exposed the civilians we pay to police and protect us to conditions approaching those into which we interject our soldiers in wartime. Partly this is due to our national security fixation since 9/11, resulting in big-city police departments with antiterrorism units that rival those of entire countries, and in the militarization of police departments large and small, with the special uniforms, weapons, and material we might formerly have associated with National Guard units. The relentless emphasis on security, the evidence that the next mass shooting can happen anywhere, the hot focus of the media on each outburst of violence, and the political necessity of making people feel safer than they are—all of these factors create for civilian law enforcers expectations similar to those that soldiers and their commanders experience. The stress produced by these expectations is one thing the police must live with, but the danger they face as they do their jobs in a militarized environment is even more consequential.

Beginning well before 9/11, Second Amendment absolutism began to make the accessibility, variety, and sheer number of powerful weapons pervasive throughout our society. Back in the late 1960s, it was possible to conclude that gun violence was essentially a black, inner-city problem, and the Gun Control Act of 1968 was intended to block the flow of cheap handguns known in racially tinged jargon as Saturday night specials. A quarter-century later, the 1994 federal assault weapons ban recognized the increasing prevalence and danger to society of military-style weapons and ammunition. It prevented the manufacture of semiautomatic assault weapons and high-capacity ammunition magazines. Former presidents Gerald Ford, Jimmy Carter, and Ronald Reagan all publicly supported the bill, which Bill Clinton signed into law. The ban lasted 10 years and expired. An attempt by President Obama to pass a new ban on assault weapons after the Sandy Hook massacre failed a Senate vote in 2013. A year ago, the U.S. Bureau of Alcohol, Tobacco, Firearms and Explosives proposed a ban on a certain type of armor-piercing bullet that has been legal to use in semiautomatic rifles. When President Reagan signed a bill banning similar sorts of bullets in 1986, he referred to these munitions as "so-called cop-killer bullets, which pose an unreasonable threat to law enforcement officers who use soft body armor." The ATF proposed to add the currently legal bullet to the ban because it can now be used in a concealable semiautomatic pistol, making it more dangerous to the police. But the ATF reversed itself even before a month-long comment period was up because the National Rifle Association mustered so many negative responses: of a total of 80,000, "the vast majority" were critical, according to the ATF. More than half the members of the House and of the Senate also spoke in opposition to the proposal.

Is there a connection between a citizenry armed with military-style weapons and the appalling acts of violence committed by some cops that have been widely publicized and rightly criticized? Every law enforcement officer working today knows that any routine traffic stop, delivery of a warrant or court order, or response to a domestic disturbance anywhere in the country involving people of any race or age can put them face to face with a weapon. Guns are everywhere, not just in the inner city. A 2014 Pew Research Center survey showed that half as many black households as white own guns, half as many urbanites own guns as do rural people, and those under 30 are far less likely to own a gun than those over 50. As the Black Lives Matter movement makes clear, it is impossible to take race out of a discussion of police violence, but it is also true that if a cop or deputy leaves the station house or sheriff's office anywhere in this country, whatever the racial or economic composition of the place where he or she works, the fear of being harmed and the tension this causes are always present.

Most police officers handle this daily threat as we expect them to, acting calmly and rationally, just as they are trained to behave in tense situations. But fear brings out the irrational, and racism is one of the irrationalities quickest to rise to the surface. Although we have a right to expect our law enforcers to be better than we are, to be more coolheaded and evenhanded, to check their prejudices at the door as they go out on their shift, we must recognize, given the stress and potential danger to which they are constantly exposed, that like the soldiers who fight in our name, the cops we pay to protect us are not all going to behave honorably. How much greater is our share of the blame when we allow our streets, residences, businesses, and in some places even our schools and churches to bristle with dangerous weapons—when we choose not to do everything we can to keep police officers as safe as possible as they go about their jobs?

One weapon that has lost much of its power in this country is the force of argument. Those who believe that the Second Amendment does not apply to individuals are not going to change the minds of, or have their minds changed by, those who believe that the Second Amendment means the government has little authority to restrict a citizen's right to bear arms. So perhaps it is also naive to think that a plea to make cops safer is going to change passionately held positions, even when the issue at hand is a sensible measure like restricting gun show loopholes on background checks.

Can anything clear away the impasse? Does any person or group of people have the power, the respect, or the moral standing to make things even a little saner? To me, saner would mean closing the background check loopholes for those who buy weapons at gun shows or on the Internet, making it harder for people with mental illness to buy guns, restoring the ban on semiautomatic weapons and large-capacity magazines, encouraging the development of smart guns that can be fired only by the owner (which would protect cops whose guns are taken from them, a major cause of police deaths), and funding the U.S. Centers for Disease Control and Prevention to study gun violence as a public health matter (something that Congress stopped the agency from doing in 1996 after the NRA suggested it was pushing for gun control). But that's just my list.

Who could advocate successfully for these modest measures, or for any measures whatsoever, especially those specifically designed to make the police, and by extension the rest of us, safer? Not President Obama or other political leaders, clearly; not Michael Bloomberg with his billions; not the families of the many victims of gun violence; not an electorate that polls show vastly favors certain measures; and not even the police chiefs of major cities, who met in Washington, D.C., last summer and called for, according to *The Washington Post*, "more stringent gun laws, including harsher penalties for gun crimes and the use of high-capacity magazines."

But this last group strikes me as having the best chance to make something happen. Not just chiefs of big-city departments but those involved in law enforcement from top to bottom. Police officers have the most to gain from sensible attempts to restrict access to dangerous weapons and munitions, and to reduce their numbers. Because they put themselves at risk each day, they have the moral authority to advocate for what will make them safer. Many of us who would like to see smarter gun laws are among the growing majority of Americans who do not own guns for hunting or sport shooting or self-defense and thus have less connection to the culture of gun ownership than previous generations did. But cops know guns and gun culture. In fact, there are police officers who oppose gun control, and some sheriffs (who are of course elected, not appointed) have said they would refuse to enforce certain new gun measures—although the term gun control means different things to different people, and polls suggest that most cops support at least some items from my wish list. And if all of those we pay to enforce our laws created, en masse, a wish list of their own, it would be hard for critics to make the slippery slope argument— the assertion that these modest steps would only be first steps because the police want to take away our weapons and repeal the Second Amendment. Nobody this side of the NRA leadership could really believe that to be true.

We need a national convention of law enforcement officials and officers, including police chiefs, police union heads, sheriffs, and deputies; the dozens of federal agencies with police powers ranging from the FBI, ATF, Drug Enforcement Administration, and Customs and Border Protection to the National Park Service and Bureau of Prisons; state police and the National Guard— everyone who carries a weapon to protect us and is at risk from weapons legally or illegally possessed. Groups representing other types of first responders, such as fire and rescue, might also participate, since they are often put at risk. The purpose of the convention would be to see what measures these groups could agree upon and to convince the rest of us that the present situation can be improved. A convention of sufficient size and scope could get the message across, and it could give political cover to elected officials and potential candidates who are willing to buck NRA intransigence for changes that large majorities of Americans would like to see. A state senator running for reelection who has been targeted by the NRA could tell voters that she values the collective wisdom of our cops over the wishes of gun lobbyists. If this possibility gave courage to even a few politicians in the middle who would like to vote with their conscience and their constituencies but are afraid of NRA backlash, many narrow votes in state legislatures and Congress could be turned around.

The sorts of changes that cops are likely to support won't in themselves stop mass murders or terrorist plots, won't keep guns out of the possession of all mentally ill people, criminals, or those who deal weapons to them. Still, these measures are bound to save the lives of some policemen. And if they make cops feel safer when they do their jobs and if that makes the small percentage of police officers who have the capacity to behave irrationally comfortable enough to keep control of their emotions more often, wouldn't this improve the lives of those protecting us, improve the lives of their families, improve the lives, black and otherwise, of those who come into contact with the police? And ultimately, wouldn't it make us all safer?

1. How would you respond to this question posed by the author?

"Is there a connection between a citizenry armed with military-style weapons and the appalling acts of violence committed by some cops that have been widely publicized and rightly criticized?"

2. Do you agree that gun control measures are best handled at the local level, with police support?

"SOME SHERIFFS PROTEST GUN RESTRICTIONS; OTHERS REFUSE TO ENFORCE THE LAWS," BY MARLENA CHERTOCK, EMILIE EATON, JACY MARMADUKE, AND SYDNEY STAVINOHA, FROM *NEWS21*, AUGUST 16, 2014

Sheriff Mike Lewis considers himself the last man standing for the people of Wicomico County.

"State police and highway patrol get their orders from the governor," the Maryland sheriff said. "I get my orders from the citizens in this county."

With more states passing stronger gun control laws, rural sheriffs across the country are taking the meaning of their age-old role as defenders of the Constitution to a new level by protesting such restrictions, News21 found.

Some are refusing to enforce the laws altogether.

Sheriffs in states like New York, Colorado and Maryland argue that some gun control laws defy the Second Amendment and threaten rural culture, for which gun ownership is often an integral component.

They're joined by groups like Oath Keepers and the Constitutional Sheriffs and Peace Officers Association, both of which encourage law enforcement officers to take a stand against gun control laws.

THE ROLE OF A SHERIFF

Lewis and some other sheriffs across the nation, most of them elected by residents of their counties, say their role puts them in the foremost position to stand up to gun laws they consider unconstitutional.

"The role of a sheriff is to be the interposer between the law and the citizen," said Maryland Delegate Don Dwyer, an Anne Arundel County Republican. "He should stand between the government and citizen in every issue pertaining to the law."

While the position of sheriff is not found in the U.S. Constitution, it is listed in state constitutions: Article XIVof Colorado's, Article XV of Delaware's, Part VII of Maryland's and Article XIII of New York's. Nearly all of America's 3,080 sheriffs are elected to their positions, whereas most state and city police top commanders are appointed.

When Lewis was president of the Maryland Sheriffs' Association, he testified with other sheriffs against the state's Firearms Safety Act (FSA) before it was enacted in 2013. One of the strictest gun laws in the nation, the act requires gun applicants to supply fingerprints and complete training to obtain a handgun license online. It bans 45 types of firearms, limits magazines to 10 rounds and outlaws gun ownership for people who have been involuntarily committed to a mental health facility.

After Lewis opposed the FSA, he said he was inundated with emails, handwritten letters, phone calls and visits from people thanking him for standing up for gun rights. He keeps a stuffed binder in his office with the laminated notes.

"I knew this was a local issue, but I also knew it had serious ramifications on the U.S. Constitution, specifically for our Second Amendment right," said Lewis, one of 24 sheriffs in the state. "It ignited fire among sheriffs throughout the state. Those in the rural areas all felt the way I did."

In New York, the state sheriff's association has publicly decried portions of the SAFE Act, legislation that broadened the definition of a banned assault weapon, outlawed magazines holding more than 10 rounds and created harsher punishments for anyone who kills a first-responder in the line of duty. The act was intended to establish background checks for ammunition sales, although that provision hasn't taken effect.

A handful of the state's 62 sheriffs have vowed not to enforce the high-capacity magazine and assault-weapon bans. One of the most vocal is Sheriff Tony Desmond of Schoharie County, population 32,000. He believes his refusal to enforce the SAFE Act won him re-election in 2013.

"If you have an (assault) weapon, which under the SAFE Act is considered illegal, I don't look at it as being illegal just because someone said it was," he said.

Desmond's deputies haven't made a single arrest related to the SAFE Act. Neither has the office of Sheriff Paul Van Blarcum of Ulster County. Van Blarcum said it's not his job to interpret the Constitution, so he'll enforce the law. But he said police should use discretion when enforcing the SAFE Act and determining whether to make arrests, as they do when administering tickets.

In Otsego County, New York, population 62,000, Sheriff Richard Devlin takes a similar approach. He enforces the SAFE Act but doesn't make it a priority.

"I feel as an elected official and a chief law enforcement officer of the county it would be irresponsible for me to say, 'I'm not going to enforce a law I personally disagree with,'" he said. "If someone uses a firearm in commission of a crime, I'm going to charge you with everything I have, including the SAFE Act. I won't do anything as far as confiscating weapons. We're not checking out registrations. People that are lawfully using a firearm for target shooting, we're not bothering those people."

Colorado made national headlines when 55 of the state's 62 sheriffs attempted to sign on as plaintiffs in a lawsuit challenging the constitutionality of several 2013 gun control bills in the state. The most-controversial measures banned magazines of more than 15 rounds and established background checks for private gun sales.

A federal judge said the sheriffs couldn't sue as elected officials, so Weld County Sheriff John Cooke and eight other sheriffs sued as private citizens. Cooke was the lead plaintiff in the lawsuit, which a federal district judge threw out in June. He and the other plaintiffs are preparing an appeal.

"It's not (the judge's) job to tell me what I can and can't enforce," Cooke said. "I'm still the one that has to say where do I put my priorities and resources? And it's not going to be there."

Cooke has won fans with his opposition. He, like Maryland's Sheriff Lewis, keeps a novel-thick stack of praise and thank-you notes in his office. He'll run for a Colorado Senate seat in November and is endorsed by the state's major gun lobby, Rocky Mountain Gun Owners.

Lewis, who is running for re-election this year, said sheriffs have a responsibility to push against what he sees as the federal government's continual encroachment on citizens' lives and rights.

"Where do we draw a line?" he asked. "I made a vow and a commitment that as long as I'm the sheriff of this county I will not allow the federal government to come in here and strip my law-abiding citizens of the right to bear arms. If they attempt to do that it will be an all-out civil war. Because I will stand toe-to-toe with my people."

But Brian Frosh, a Maryland state senator and an FSA sponsor and gun-control advocate of Montgomery County, said Lewis' understanding of a sheriff's role is flawed.

"If you are a sheriff in Maryland you must take an oath to uphold the law and the Constitution," said Frosh, now the Democratic nominee for Maryland attorney general. "You can't be selective. It's not up to a sheriff to decide what's constitutional and what isn't. That's what our courts are for."

Bronx County, New York, Sen. Jeffrey Klein, who co-sponsored the SAFE Act, agreed that sheriffs who refuse to enforce laws they disagree with are acting out of turn. Constitutional sheriffs are not lawyers or judges, Frosh said, which means they are following their convictions instead of the Constitution.

"We had lots of people come in (to testify against the bill) and without any basis say, 'This violates the Second Amendment,'" Frosh said. "They can cite the Second Amendment, but they couldn't explain why this violates it. And the simple fact is it does not. There is a provision of our Constitution that gives people rights with respect to firearms, but it's not as expansive as many of these people think."

But sheriffs have the power to nullify, or ignore, a law if it is unconstitutional, Maryland Delegate Dwyer said. He said James Madison referred to nullification as the rightful remedy for the Constitution.

"The sheriffs coming to testify on the bill understood the issue enough and were brave enough to come to Annapolis and make the bold stand that on their watch, in their county, they would not enforce these laws even if they passed," said Dwyer, who has recognized the sheriffs for their courage. "That is the true role and responsibility of what the sheriff is."

RURAL VERSUS URBAN DIVIDE

Some rural sheriffs argue that gun control laws are more than just unconstitutional — they're unnecessary and irrelevant. In towns and villages where passers-by stop to greet deputies and call local law enforcement to ask for help complying with gun laws, they say, firearms are less associated with crime than they are with a hunting and shooting culture that dates back to when the communities were founded.

Edward Amelio, a deputy in Lewis County, New York, shares that sentiment. There's no normal day for Amelio, who has patrolled the 27,000-person county for eight years. But he usually responds to domestic disputes, burglaries and car accidents. That's why he considers the SAFE Act unnecessary.

"We issue orders of protection and some contain a clause the judge puts in there saying a person's guns are to be confiscated," Amelio said. "That's mostly when we deal with guns."

Zachary Reinhart, a deputy sheriff in Schoharie County, New York, said he responds to a wide variety of calls, too.

"Our calls range from accidental 911 dials to domestic disputes to bar fights," he said. "You can't really typify a day at the Schoharie County Sheriff's Office. It's all pretty helter-skelter."

Violent crime also isn't common in Wicomico County, Maryland, where Lewis is sheriff. He receives daily shooting reports from the Maryland Coordination and Analysis Center, which are not available for public disclosure.

"You always see 'nothing to report' in the eastern region, in the southern region, in the northern region, in the western region," Lewis said. "But the Baltimore central region? Homicide after homicide after homicide."

Even though there are few gun crimes in rural areas, Sheriff Michael Carpinelli in Lewis County argues that people need guns for self-defense.

"People rely on the police in an urban environment to come and protect you all the time," he said. "People who live in a rural area also rely upon the police, but they realize that they live further out from those resources and that they may have to take action themselves."

Duke law professor Joseph Blocher said gun culture has varied in urban and rural areas for centuries.

"It has long been the case that gun use and ownership and gun culture are concentrated in rural areas, whereas support for gun control and efforts to curb gun violence are concentrated in urban areas," he said. "In the last couple decades we've moved away from that towards a more-centralized gun control."

Lewis bemoaned lawmakers who craft gun-control legislation but are ignorant about guns. "They have no idea between a long gun and a handgun," he said. "Many of them admittedly have never fired a weapon in their lives."

But Klein, the Bronx County senator, said he does understand the gun and hunting culture in upstate New York.

"Growing up, my father was in the military," Klein said. "When I was younger, I had a .22-caliber gun. In the past, I've gone pheasant hunting, quail hunting. It's great," he said. "I mean, there's nothing that we do in Albany, especially with the SAFE Act, that in any way takes away someone's right to own a gun for hunting purposes."

OATH KEEPERS AND CSPOA

If former Arizona sheriff Richard Mack had it his way, there wouldn't be a single gun control law in the U.S.

"I studied what the Founding Fathers meant about the Second Amendment, the right to keep and bear arms, and the conclusion is inescapable," said Mack, the founder of the Constitutional Sheriffs and Peace Officers Association (CSPOA). "There's no way around it. Gun control in America is against the law."

He knows his no-compromise stance has cost him and the CSPOA the support of some sheriffs and law enforcement organizations around the country. And it's resulted in civil rights agencies labeling CSPOA an anti-government "patriot group."

But Mack, the former sheriff in eastern Arizona's rural Graham County, is not letting up. His conviction is central to the ideology of CSPOA, which he founded in 2011 to "unite all public servants and sheriffs, to keep their word to uphold, defend, protect, preserve and obey" the Constitution, according to his introduction letter on the association's website.

CSPOA also has ties to Oath Keepers, an organization founded in 2009 with a similar goal to unite veterans, law enforcement officers and first-responders who pledge to keep their oath to "defend the Constitution against all enemies, foreign and domestic." Mack serves on the Oath Keepers Board of Directors.

Oath Keepers is larger and farther-reaching than CSPOA, with active chapters in 48 states and the District of Columbia, and an estimated national membership of 40,000. Its website features a declaration of "orders we will not obey," including those to disarm Americans, impose martial law on a state and blockade cities.

CSPOA grabbed media attention in February with a growing list of sheriffs — 484 as of late July — professing opposition to federal gun control. Detailed with links beside each name, the sheriffs' stances run the gamut from refusals to impose a litany of federal and state gun-control laws, to vague vows to protect their constituents' Second Amendment rights, to law critiques that stop short of promising noncompliance.

Only 16 of those 484 are listed as CSPOA members.

Some sheriffs perceive Oath Keepers and CSPOA as too radical to associate with. Desmond, of Schoharie County, New York, is known around his state for openly not enforcing provisions of the SAFE Act that he considers unconstitutional. Still, he's not a member of either organization.

"I understand where they are, I guess, but I just have to worry right here myself," Desmond said. "I don't want to get involved with somebody that may be a bit more proactive when it comes to the SAFE Act. I want to have the image that I protect gun owners, but I'm not fanatical about it."

Mack is familiar with that sentiment. He suspects it's hindered the growth of CSPOA.

"This is such a new idea for so many sheriffs that it's hard for them to swallow it," Mack said. "They've fallen into the brainwashing and the mainstream ideas that you just have to go after the drug dealers and the

DUIs and serve court papers — and that the federal government is the supreme law of the land."

The Southern Poverty Law Center, a civil rights nonprofit that classifies and combats hate and extremist groups, included both CSPOA and Oath Keepers on its list of 1,096 anti-government "patriot" groups active in 2013. Both groups have faced criticism for their alleged connections to people accused of crimes that range from possessing a live napalm bomb to shooting and killing two Las Vegas police officers and a bystander in June.

Media representatives from the Southern Poverty Law Center did not return phone calls and emails requesting comment.

Franklin Shook, an Oath Keepers board member who goes by the pseudonym "Elias Alias," said the organization doesn't promote violence, but rather a message of peaceful noncompliance.

"What Oath Keepers is saying is ... when you get an order to go to somebody's house and collect one of these guns, just stand down," Shook said. "Say peacefully, 'I refuse to carry out an unlawful order,' and we, the organization, will do everything in our power to keep public pressure on your side to keep you from getting in trouble for standing down. That makes Oath Keepers extremely dangerous to the system."

THE FUTURE OF GUN CONTROL LAWS

Self-proclaimed constitutional sheriffs hope that courts will oust gun control measures in their states — but they recognize that may not happen. Lawsuits challenging the constitutionality of gun control legislation in Maryland, New York and Colorado have been, for the most part, unsuccessful.

In New York, five SAFE Act-related lawsuits have yielded few results: One lawsuit resulted in an expansion of the magazine limit from seven rounds to 10, but the rest of the measures were thrown out and are awaiting appeal; a similar lawsuit was stayed; a third was thrown out and denied appeal; and two additional lawsuits have been combined but are stagnating in court.

Plaintiffs in the Colorado sheriff lawsuit are preparing to appeal the decision of a federal district judge who in June upheld the constitutionality of the 2013 gun control laws.

A lawsuit seeking to overturn Maryland's assault weapons and high-capacity magazine bans went to trial in July, but the judge has yet to issue a ruling.

"My hope is that the governor will look at it now that it's been a year plus and say, 'We've had some provisions that have failed. Let's sit down and look at this and have a meaningful conversation.'" New York's Devlin said. "I personally don't see that happening, but I'd like to see that happen."

1. If local law enforcement refuses to enforce gun control laws, how might the federal and state governments regulate these laws more effectively?

CONCLUSION

To end on a hopeful note, the terrifying epidemic of gun violence of late has focused increased attention on progressive voices within the gun debate— surely an encouraging development. Groups such as the Brady Campaign, politicians such as New York Senator Charles Schumer (D), and even comedians such as Amy Schumer (Charles's cousin) have placed gun safety at the center of their disparate agendas.

Demographic shifts are also encouraging. People under the age of thirty-five are far less likely to own guns. As a generational shift occurs, it is possible that hardline gun advocates will simply die off, leaving more public health minded people in charge of gun policy going forward.

Still, the approximately 270 million guns in America are not going anywhere. Even the most radical gun control advocates concede that law-abiding citizens will always have a right to bear arms in self-defense; Obama is not coming for anyone's guns. But we have work to do if we wish to pass even "common-sense" gun legislation. The NRA and other "no-compromise" gun-rights groups purchase immense lobbying power, disproportionate even to the support of its base. Thus, even modest reforms have failed to make it through Congress recently.

For this reason, local ordinances may be the best bulwark against gun violence. The Supreme Court has routinely refused to hear cases on the minutiae of gun laws. Given enough grassroots support, rational gun laws can therefore easily be instituted. We hope you'll be part of this movement. Too many lives have already been lost due to America's senseless love for firearms.

ABOUT THE EDITOR

Anne Cunningham has a PhD in Comparative Literature, and has published articles on women modernist writers and feminist theory. She currently works as an Instructor of English at the University of New Mexico—Taos. She is also a songwriter and performer, and lives with her husband and music partner David Lerner in Arroyo Hondo, NM.

BIBLIOGRAPHY

Arnold, Meg and Nathan Goodman. "How Gun Control Hurts Minorities: Progressives Turn Their Backs on Those Most Vulnerable to Expanded Police Powers." *PanAm Post*, October 13, 2015. (https://panampost.com/valerie-marsman/2015/10/13/how-gun-control-hurts-minorities).

Bartels, Lynn. "Two States, Same Challenge: Lawmakers In Colorado And Connecticut Made Tough Calls In The Wake Of Mass Shootings." The National Conference of State Legislatures. *State Legislatures*, 39.7, 2013. (http://www.ncsl.org/portals/1/documents/magazine/articles/2013/sl_0713-twostates.pdf).

Blackman, Josh. "Our Gun-Shy Justices: The Supreme Court Abandons The Second Amendment." *The American Spectator*, June 23, 2014. (http://spectator.org/59552_our-gun-shy-justices).

Burrus, Trevor. "Why the Gun Debate Never Ends." The Foundation for Economic Freedom, June 28, 2016. (https://fee.org/articles/why-the-gun-debate-never-ends).

Chertock, Marlena et al. "Some Sheriffs Protest Gun Restrictions; Others Refuse to Enforce the Laws." *News21*, August 16, 2014. (http://gunwars.news21.com/2014/some-sheriffs-protest-gun-restrictions-others-refuse-to-enforce-laws).

DeBrabander, Firmin. "Our Armed Society: The Common Good Is The First Victim Of America's Gun Culture." *America*, September 14, 2015. (http://americamagazine.org/issue/our-armed-society).

Eichenwald, Kurt. "Americans Don't Have The Right To Bear Just Any Arms; There Is An Easy Solution To America's Arguments About Gun Control, But The Childish Extremists On Both Sides Need To Leave The Room." *Newsweek*, July 24, 2015. (http://www.newsweek.com/2015/07/24/americans-mass-shootings-assault-weapons-right-bear-arms-354203.html).

Feffer, John. "Guys with Guns: The U.S. Government Should Be Making it More Difficult to Sell Weapons—At Home as Well as Abroad." *Foreign Policy in Focus*, June 18, 2014. (http://fpif.org/guys-guns).

Ferris, Kirby. "Kirby Ferris Interviews Aaron Zelman." Jews for the Preservation of Firearm Ownership, 2009. (http://jpfo. org/filegen-a-m/az-kf-interview.htm).

Hutson, Jonathan and John Lott. "Debate: Is Strict Gun Control the Best Way to Prevent Shootings? Another Massacre Begs What Can Be Done." *PanAm Post*, June 30, 2015. (https://panampost.com/editor/2015/06/30/is-strict-gun-control-the-best-way-to-prevent-shootings).

Lanciel, Alex and Jim Tuttle. "Citing the Constitution, Groups Prepare to Defend Themselves and Their Rights." *News21*

Lytton, Timothy D. "Sandy Hook Lawsuit is Latest Effort to Hold Gun Makers Liable for Mass Shootings." *The Conversation.*

Masters, Jonathan. "U.S. Gun Policy: Global Comparisons." The Council on Foreign Relations, January 12, 2016. (http://www. cfr.org/society-and-culture/us-gun-policy-global-comparisons/p29735).

McDaniel, Justine et al. "Eight States Have Passed Laws Voiding Federal Firearms Regulations." *News21*, (http://gunwars. news21.com/2014/eight-states-have-passed-laws-voiding-federal-firearms-regulations).

McDaniel, Justine et al. "Debate Has Changed since Newtown, But Not Always in Predictable Ways." *News21*, August 16, 2014. (http://gunwars.news21.com/2014/debate-has-changed-since-newtown-but-not-always-in-predictable-ways).

Newport, Frank. "American Public Opinion and Guns." Gallup, December 4, 2015. (http://www.gallup.com/opinion/polling-matters/187511/american-public-opinion-guns.aspx).

O'Brien, Kerry et al. "Racism, Gun Ownership and Gun Control: Biased Attitudes in US Whites May Influence Policy Decisions." *FPLoS One*, October 31, 2013. (http://journals. plos.org/plosone/article?id=10.1371/journal.pone.0077552).

Parker, Jonathan. "Explainer: What is the 2nd Amendment and How Does it Impact US Gun Control?" *The Conversation*, June 15, 2016. (https://theconversation.com/explainer-what-is-the-2nd-amendment-and-how-does-it-impact-us-gun-control-61068).

Queally, John. "Democrat-Controlled Senate Fails to Pass Even 'Watered-Down, Over-Compromised' Gun Legislation." *Common Dreams*, August 17, 2013. (http://www.common-dreams.org/news/2013/04/17/democrat-controlled-senate-fails-pass-even-watered-down-over-compromised-gun).

Reisenwitz, Cathy. "Think Gays Don't Need Gun Rights? Check Your Privilege." The Foundation for Economic Freedom, June 28, 2016. (https://fee.org/articles/think-gays-dont-need-gun-rights-check-your-privilege).

Salzman, Jason. "Media Silence on an Irate Gun Company's Connection to Sandy Hook: How is Adam Lanza Not Part of This Story?" *OtherWords*, January 29, 2014. (http://otherwords.org/media-silence-irate-gun-companys-connection-sandy-hook).

VerBruggen, Robert. "Fewer Guns, Less Homicide? If Only It Were So Simple." *National Review*, December 21, 2015. (https://www.nationalreview.com/nrd/articles/427936/fewer-guns-less-homicide).

Wahowiak, Lindsey. "Public Health Taking Stronger Approach To Gun Violence: APHA, Brady Team Up On Prevention." *The Nation's Health*, January 2016. (http://thenationshealth.aphapublications.org/content/45/10/1.3.full).

Wilson, Robert. "Common Sense: It's Time For Police Officers To Start Demanding Gun Laws That Could End Up Saving Their Own Lives." *The American Scholar*, February 28, 2016. (https://theamericanscholar.org/common-sense).

Wogan, J.B. "Beyond Gun Control: Precluded From Banning The Ownership Of Firearms, Cities Are Finding New Ways To Go After Gun Violence." *Governing*, September 2014. (http://www.governing.com/topics/public-justice-safety/gov-cities-new-way-gun-violence.html).

CHAPTER NOTES

CHAPTER 1: WHAT THE EXPERTS SAY

EXCERPT FROM "RACISM, GUN OWNERSHIP AND GUN CONTROL: BIASED ATTITUDES IN US WHITES MAY INFLUENCE POLICY DECISIONS," BY KERRY O'BRIEN, WALTER FORREST, DERMOT LYNOTT, AND MICHAEL DALY

1. Hoyert DL, Xu J (2012) Deaths: preliminary data for 2011. Natl Vital Stat Rep 61: 1–65 [PubMed]

2. UN Office on Drugs and Crimes website. United Nations surveys on crime trends and the operations of criminal justice systems. Available: www.unodc.org/documents/data-and-analysis/statistics/Homicide/Homicides_by_fire-arms.xls Accessed 2013 May 5.

3. Smith TW (2001) National gun policy survey of the national opinion research centre: Research findings. Chicago: University of Chicago, National Opinion Research Center.

4. Pew Research Center (2013) Perspectives of Gun Owners, Non-Owners: Why Own a Gun? Protection Is Now Top Reason. Pew Research Center. http://www.people-press.org/2013/03/12/why-own-a-gun-protection-is-now-top-reason/Accessed 27/03/2013.

5. Lott JR (2010) More guns, less crime: Understanding crime and gun-control laws. 3rd ed. Chicago: University of Chicago Press.

6. Kellermann AL, Rivara FP, Rushforth NB, Banton JG, Reay DT, et al. (1993) Gun ownership as a risk factor for homicide in the home. N Engl J Med 329: 1084–91 [PubMed]

7. Kellermann AL, Rivara FP, Somes G, Reay DT, Francisco J, et al. (1992) Suicide in the home in relation to gun ownership. N Engl J Med 327: 467–72 [PubMed]

8. Chapman S, Alpers P, Agho K, Jones M (2006) Australia's 1996 gun law reforms: faster falls in firearm deaths, firearm suicides, and a decade without mass shootings. Inj Prev 12: 365–372[PMC free article] [PubMed]

9. Leenaars AA, Moksony F, Lester D, Wenckstern S (2003) The impact of gun control (Bill C-51) on suicide in Canada. Death Stud 27: 103–124 [PubMed]

10. Leigh A, Neill C (2012) Do gun buybacks save lives? Evidence from panel data. Am Law Econ Rev 12: 462–508

11. McCarthy M (2013) Reviving research into US gun violence. BMJ 346: f980. [PubMed]

12. Davies E (2013) If guns don't kill people, ignorance might. BMJ 346: f1058

13. Winkler A (2011) Gunfight: The Battle Over the Right to Bear Arms in America. New York, N.Y. London: W.W. Norton.

14. Pew Research Center (2013) Gun Rights Proponents More Politically Active: In Gun Control Debate, Several Options Draw Majority Support. Pew Research Center http://www. people-press.org/files/legacy-pdf/01-14-13%20Gun%20Policy%20Release.pdf Accessed 18/05/2013.

15. Benforado A (2010) Quick on the draw: Implicit bias and the second amendment. Oregon Law Rev 89: 1–81

16. Kleck G, Kovandzic T, Saber M, Hauser W (2010) The effect of perceived risk and victimization on plans to purchase a gun for self-protection J Crim Just. 39: 312–319

17. Sears DO, Henry PJ (2005) Over thirty years later: A contemporary look at symbolic racism. Adv Exp Soc Psychol 37: 95–150

18. Barkan S, Cohn SE (2005) Why Whites Favor Spending More Money to Fight Crime: The Role of Racial Prejudice. Soc Probl 52: 300–315

19. Hurwitz J, Peffley M (1997) Public Perceptions of Race and Crime: The Role of Racial Stereotypes. Am J Polit Sci 41: 374–401

20. Kahan DM, Braman D (2002) More Statistics, Less Persuasion: A Cultural Theory of Gun-Risk Perceptions. U Penn Law Rev 151: 1291

21. Greenwald AG, Poehlman TA, Uhlmann EL, Banaji MR (2003) Understanding and using the Implicit Association Test: III. Meta-analysis of predictive validity. J Pers Soc Psychol 97: 17–41[PubMed]

22. Lane KA, Kang J, Banaji MR (2007) Implicit social cognition and law. Annu Rev Law Soc Sci 3: 427–451

23. Knowles ED, Lowery BS, Schaumberg RL (2010) Racial prejudice predicts opposition to Obama and his health care reform plan. J Exp Soc Psy 46: 420–423

24. Henderson M, Hillygus DS (2011) The Dynamics of Health Care Opinion, 2008–2010: Partisanship, Self-Interest, and Racial Resentment. J Health Polit Pol Law 36: 945–960 [PubMed]

25. Rabinowitz JL, Sears DO, Sidanius J, Krosnick JA (2009) Why do white Americans oppose race-targeted policies? Clarifying the impact of symbolic racism. Polit Psychol 30: 805–828[PMC free article] [PubMed]

26. Campbell A (1971) White attitudes toward black people. Ann Arbor: Institute for Social Research, University of Michigan.

27. Crosby F, Bromley S, Saxe L (1980) Recent unobtrusive studies of Black and White discrimination and prejudice: A literature review. Psychol Bull 87: 546–563

28. McConahay J (1986) Modern racism, ambivalence, and the Modern Racism Scale. In J. Gaertner & S. Dovidio (Eds.), Prejudice, discrimination and racism. Orlando, FL. Academic Press. 91–125.

29. Sears DO, Henry PJ (2003) The origins of symbolic racism. J Pers Soc Psychol 85: 259–275[PubMed]

30. Chiricos T, Welch K, Gertz M (2004) Racial typification of crime and support for punitive measures. Criminology 42: 359–390

31. Berg JA (2013) Opposition to Pro-Immigrant Public Policy: Symbolic Racism and Group Threat. Soc Inq 83: 1–31

32. Tarman C, Sears DO (2005) The conceptualization and measurement of symbolic racism. J Polit63: 731–761

33. Sears D, Van Laar C, Carillo M, Kosterman R (1997) Is it really racism? The origins of White Americans' opposition to race-targeted policies. Public Opin Quart 61: 16–53

34. Green EGT, Staerklé C, Sears DO (2006) Symbolic racism and whites' attitudes towards punitive and preventive crime policies. Law Human Behav 30: 435–54 [PubMed]

35. DeBell M, Krosnick JA, Lupia A (2010) Methodology Report and User Guide for the 2008–2009 ANES Panel Study. Stanford Univ. and Univ. Michigan.

36. Nicholson SP, Segura GM (2012) Who's the Party of the People? Economic Populism and the U.S. Public's Beliefs About Political Parties. Political Behavior 34: 369–389

37. Henry PJ, Sears DO (2002) The Symbolic Racism 2000 Scale. Polit Psychol 23: 253–283

38. Kleck G (1996) Crime, Culture Conflict and the Sources of Support for Gun Control: A Multilevel Application of the General Social Surveys. Am Behav Sci 39: 387–404

39. Blanton H, Jaccard J, Klick J, Mellers B, Mitchell G, et al. (2009) Strong claims and weak evidence: reassessing the predictive validity of the IAT. J Appl Psychol 94: 567–582 [PubMed]

40. Mitchell G, Tetlock PE (2006) Antidiscrimination law and the perils of mindreading. Ohio State Law J 67: 1023–1121

41. Rothermund K, Wentura D, De Houwer J (2005) Validity of the salience asymmetry account of the Implicit Association Test: Reply to Greenwald, Nosek, Banaji, and Klauer (2005). J Exper Psychol: Gen 134: 426–430 [PubMed]

42. Vanman EJ, Saltz JL, Nathan LR, Warren JA (2004) Racial discrimination by low prejudiced Whites: Facial movements as implicit measures of attitudes related to behavior. Psychol Science 11: 711–714 [PubMed]

43. Rezaei AR (2011) Validity and Reliability of the IAT: Measuring Gender and Ethnic Stereotypes.Comput Human Behav 27: 1937–1941

44. Sabin JA, Nosek BA, Greenwald AG, Rivara FP (2009) Physicians' implicit and explicit attitudes about race by MD race, ethnicity, and gender. J Health Care Poor Underserved 20: 896–913[PMC free article] [PubMed]

45. Kinder DR, Ryan TJ (2012) Prejudice and Politics Re-Examined: The Political Significance of Implicit Racial Bias. Prepared for the annual meeting of the American Political Science Association. New Orleans.

46. Klinesmith J, Kasser T, McAndrew FT (2006) Guns, Testosterone, and Aggression An Experimental Test of a Mediational Hypothesis. Psychol Science 17: 568–571 [PubMed]

47. Felson R, Paré P (2010) Firearms and Fisticuffs: Region, Race, and Adversary Effects on Homicide and Assault. Soc Sci Res 39: 272–284

48. Tang H, Cowling DW, Lloyd JC, Rogers T, Koumjian KL, et al. (2003) Changes of attitudes and patronage behaviors in response to a smoke-free bar law. J Information 93: 611–617[PMC free article] [PubMed]

49. Heloma A, Jaakkola MS (2003) Four year follow up of smoke exposure, attitudes and smoking behaviour following enactment of Finland's national smoke free work place law. Addiction 98: 1111–1117 [PubMed]

assault weapon A fluid category of semi-automatic firearms, currently lacking a precise definition. Generally taken to mean powerful weapons designed for military conflict, these are largely classified by their cosmetic, as opposed to functional, characteristics.

Assault Weapon Ban of 1994 Ban focusing on eighteen specific semi-automatic firearms and high-capacity magazines. Under this law, it was illegal to manufacture these guns for civilian use. The ban expired in 2004 after ten years, and was not renewed.

automatic Any weapon that uses cartridges and fires automatically as long as ammunition is in the feed system. Includes machine guns, submachine guns, and assault rifles.

barrel The tube through which the bullet or shot passes.

Brady Handgun Violence Prevention Act of 1993 (Brady Bill) Effective congressional act requiring a background check on all purchasers of firearms. After a five-day waiting period, those with no record of mental illness or criminal records were cleared for purchase. Since 1998, the waiting period has been reduced to forty-eight hours.

caliber A measure of the diameter of a firearm's bore (internal part of the barrel that the bullet passes through). Can be noted as fractions of inches or millimeters.

firearm A gun that uses gunpowder as its propellant, as opposed to air guns or other firing systems.

Gun Control Act of 1968 Mandated the Federal Firearms Licensing system for gun dealers, and regulated interstate trade of guns. Also set stipulations on who could lawfully possess a gun.

gunshow loophole A gunshow loophole (so named because this loophole is often legally exploited at gun shows) denotes the private sale of weapons from one owner to another who wouldn't otherwise qualify if given a background check.

r shotgun with a long barrel used primar-
ame, which is designed to be fired against

Firearms Act of 1934 The act that imposed taxation
firearms and regulated their interstate transportation.

National Instant Criminal Background Check (NICS) The
system that checks a potential gun buyers' name and birth
record against several databases. If the person is determined
to be ineligible, the sale is illegal.

National Rifle Association (NRA) The largest and most powerful gun lobby group advocating broad and uncompromising
rights for gun owners.

shotgun A long gun that fires a group of pellets called shot,
rather than a single bullet.

silencer An external devise that mutes the sound of gunfire.

waiting period A delay between the purchase of a firearm and
its delivery in which background checks and other legal
safeguards take place, which can be anywhere from forty-
eight hours to five days.

FOR MORE INFORMATI

BOOKS

Barrett, Paul. *Glock: The Rise of America's Gun*. London: Crown, 2013.

Beck, Glenn. *Control: Exposing the Truth about Guns*. New York: Mercury Editions, 2013.

Cook, Philip. *The Gun Debate: What Everyone Needs to Know*. New York: Oxford University Press, 2014.

Haag, Pamela. *The Gunning of America: Business and the Making of American Gun Culture*. New York: Perseus, 2016.

Kyle, Chris. *American Gun: A History of the U.S. in Ten Firearms*. New York: Harper Collins, 2013.

Lott, John. *More Guns, Less Crime: Understanding Crime and Gun Control Laws*. Chicago, IL: University of Chicago Press, 2010

Waldman, Michal. *The Second Amendment: A Biography*. New York: Simon & Schuster, 2015.

Webster, Daniel. *Reducing Gun Violence in America: Informing Policy with Evidence and Analysis.* Baltimore, MD: Johns Hopkins University Press, 2013.

Whitney, Craig. *Living With Guns: A Liberal's Case for the Second Amendment.* New York: Public Affairs, 2012.

Winkler, Adam. *Gunfight: The Battle Over the Right to Bear Arms in America*. New York: WW Norton & Co., 2013.

WEBSITES

ᴏr Gun Control
..org

..ɳzed by former New York City mayor Michael Bloomberg,
this group advocates for safer communities from a local
level. Their site points the way to easy ways citizens can get
involved with this issue, or simply inform themselves.

American Progress on Gun Violence
www.americanprogress.org/tag/gun-violence/view
Reports, fact sheets, and issue briefs on all facets of gun
  control can be found at this site, which is generally written
  from a progressive angle.

Gun Owners of America
www.gunowners.org
Gun Owners of America is a self-described "no-compromise"
  gun advocacy group. Predictably, their website presents only
  material from this dogmatic point of view, and a prominent
  "take action" section for gun owners to get involved.